358

D0455110

CENTRAL LIBRARY
828 "I" STREET
SACRAMENTO, CA 95814
APR   2001

Swimming with Giants

Swimming with Giants

My Encounters with Whales,
Dolphins, and Seals

ANNE COLLET

with Marc Sich

Translated by Gayle Wurst

MILKWEED EDITIONS

© 1998, Librairie Plon
© 2000, Translation by Gayle Wurst
This book was originally published in 1998 under the title *Danse avec les baleines*.

All rights reserved. Except for brief quotations in critical articles or reviews, no part of this book may be reproduced in any manner without prior written permission from the publisher: Milkweed Editions, 1011 Washington Avenue South, Suite 300, Minneapolis, Minnesota 55415/(800) 520-6455/www.milkweed.org/www.worldashome.org

Published 2000 by Milkweed Editions
Printed in the United States of America
Jacket photo composition by Sally Wagner, Sally J. Wagner, Inc.
Jacket photo of whale by Izzy Schwartz, Photo Disc
Jacket photo of scuba diver by Ian Cartwright, Photo Disc
Photos on back of jacket and jacket flaps courtesy of Anne Collet
Interior design by Donna Burch
The text of this book is set in Centaur.
00 01 02 03 04   5 4 3 2 1
First Edition

Milkweed Editions, a nonprofit publisher, gratefully acknowledges support from our World As Home funders: Lila Wallace-Reader's Digest Fund; Creation and Presentation programs of the National Endowment for the Arts; and Reader's Legacy underwriter Elly Sturgis. Other support has been provided by the Elmer L. and Eleanor J. Andersen Foundation; James Ford Bell Foundation; Bush Foundation; General Mills Foundation; Honeywell Foundation; Jerome Foundation; McKnight Foundation; Minnesota State Arts Board through an appropriation by the Minnesota State Legislature; Norwest Foundation on behalf of Norwest Bank Minnesota; Lawrence and Elizabeth Ann O'Shaughnessy Charitable Income Trust in honor of Lawrence M. O'Shaughnessy; Oswald Family Foundation; Ritz Foundation on behalf of Mr. and Mrs. E. J. Phelps Jr.; John and Beverly Rollwagen Fund of the Minneapolis Foundation; St. Paul Companies, Inc.; Star Tribune Foundation; Target Foundation on behalf of Dayton's, Mervyn's California, and Target Stores; U.S. Bancorp Piper Jaffray Foundation on behalf of U.S. Bancorp Piper Jaffray; and generous individuals.

Library of Congress Cataloging-in-Publication Data

Collet, Anne.
    [Danse avec les baleines. English]
    Swimming with Giants : my encounters with whales, dolphins, and seals / Anne Collet with Marc Sich ; translated by Gayle Wurst.— 1st ed.
      p. cm.
    ISBN 1-57131-244-7 (cloth)
    1. Collet, Anne. 2. Women marine mammalogists—France—Biography. 3. Marine mammalogists—France—Biography. 4. Whales. I. Sich, Marc. II. Title.

QH91.3.C66 A3 2000
599.5'092—dc21
[B]   00-021056

This book is printed on acid-free, recycled paper.

For Greg Donovan, Sir Richard Harrison,
Christina Lockyer, Bill Perrin, and Ian Stirling

It is thanks to my encounters with these scientists,
now friends, who always answered my questions with care and
patience, that I have been lucky enough to encounter whales
and dolphins, which in their turn, posed questions to me.

Swimming with Giants

Introduction

It seems only a few years ago that I first met Anne, when we were both young biologists attending a conference in California on reproduction in whales, dolphins, and porpoises. Now, almost twenty years later, Anne still has the same warmth and enthusiasm for marine mammals that she had then, and I feel very proud to be asked to write an introduction to her book. I must confess that this is not the kind of book I would normally read about cetaceans—but this one avoids all the pitfalls that can affect "popular" books on whales. What comes across is neither a self-penned eulogy nor a polemic against the evils of the world. It is simply a book that expresses not only the wonder but also the tenderness that encounters with whales engender. The original title of the French edition of the book made a semihumorous reference to the film *Dances with Wolves.* The atmosphere of this book, and of Anne, is of "Smiling with Whales"—and smiling inside is indeed the most common reaction when encountering whales and dolphins in the wild. It is a strong, warm feeling and especially welcome on a cold, gray, windy day on the open ocean. In fact, it is the same reaction that encounters with Anne engender!

Greg Donovan
International Whaling Commission

Swimming with Giants

Uncle Jacques and the Chocolate Cream Puffs

E very family in Brittany has a son who is a sailor. And every good family in Brittany has a son in the Royal Navy—preferably, an officer. Maybe this would have been me, if I hadn't been born a girl. I doubt I could have conformed to military discipline, but I dreamed about it briefly when I was ten years old. It was all Uncle Jacques's fault—Uncle Jacques with his uniforms, his love of bicycles, and his generous way of buying me little pastries.

I was born in Paris only by happenstance. From Dunkerque on my father's side and Brest on my mother's, I came into this world imbued with the love of the sea. My parents fueled this passion to fiery heights on vacations, when they carried us off—my two older brothers, my younger sister, and me—to the beaches of Alderney and the Crozon Peninsula. Whenever I recall these trips to Brittany, I still can hear my mother crying: "Anne! Get out of the water right now! You're completely blue!"

From morning to night, I paddled and splashed, then splashed and paddled some more. I went swimming when the tide came in and followed it when it went out, collecting crabs from water holes, capturing shrimp, prying off limpets stuck to the rocks. I used these poor mollusks as green crab bait, threading them on a safety pin at the end of a piece of string, and made necklaces from their shells. The crabs I hung up on the children's beach house to dry in the sun. This was how I spent my phase of childhood cruelty; it was my way of pulling the wings off flies.

We waded in shores of abundance. In half an hour, my sister and I would fill a basket with five quarts of *praires* and *palourdes*, two kinds of local clams, which we traded for delicious *carambars*—ten of them, at five centimes apiece. A similar harvest today would take two adults an entire morning. I also adored hunting for tough old mollusks called *couteaux*. We sprinkled a little salt over their holes, and waited for them to come out. It was magic. Of course, no one ate them, not even the dogs; their flesh was much too rubbery. Now they are served up in restaurants as a "typical" regional dish.

I loved the water that chapped my skin, the waves that rolled the soft-sounding shingle, the wind that tangled my hair, and the sea spray that stuck it together. I even loved the bottom slime that penetrated, cold and viscous, through a hole in my boot. Some people found the smell of it nauseating, but not me. To me it smelled like the sea.

Later, I loved the ocean because it could be such a wonderful playground. The sea is never so beautiful as when it is full of bristling white sails. When my brother Antoine started sixth grade, our parents offered him a little dinghy equipped with a scull. I stole off with it as often as possible. A boat! A boat is freedom, and what pride I felt at eight years old as the only master on board! But seafaring adventures were only for boys, not girls, everyone explained to me. And, of course, freedom was for them too. I quickly understood that the "weaker" sex had to battle for its own.

Paris was school and restrictions, tiredness, dissension, gloomy winter mornings going down the metro steps beneath the drizzling rain. My mother worked a lot, much too much. An ophthalmologist, she rushed from one clinic to the next from morning till night, day in and day out. We were handed over to a succession of au pairs, first in Montmartre where we lived for a long time, then in the Latin Quarter. I was ten when we moved there in the middle of the 1960s. In my heart, I rebelled against Paris. I would dream of the coast of Brittany, of sailboats tacking between the tip of Saint-Mathieu and Ushant Island. I drew pictures of my dreams, and did it well, it seems—I was even said to have talent— and felt bored. Except at my Uncle Jacques's house.

Uncle Jacques was the glory of our family. My mother's older brother, Jacques Vichot was a Breton living in Paris, an officer in the Royal Navy, and a founder of the Marine Museum. His wife, Régine, was my godmother, and they both adored me. They invited me to their house—all by myself! It was the height of luxury, a delight! I was the center of all their attention: no brothers, no sister. For the space of an afternoon, I was their darling, and it pleased me more than anything else in the world.

Régine and Jacques had a fabulous apartment on the top floor of the Chaillot Palace, which houses the Musée de la Marine in Paris, and an immense terrace with a view of the Trocadero gardens. On Sundays when I went to visit them, they pampered me and let me do whatever I pleased. More than anything else, I loved to see my uncle dressed in his formal uniform. He was superb—tall, elegantly slender, strong, a beautiful figure of a man. He also had good taste. A bit of an artist himself, he had taken up painting in his leisure time, and he evaluated my drawings like a connoisseur. I remember one of his designs, used today as an emblem in marine museums all over France: a motif with two "sea horses," one on either side of a cannon. Rather than the usual equipage, his horses had mermaids' tails. Everyone thinks the emblem was taken from an eighteenth-century ship, but it's actually a legacy from Uncle Jacques.

With my aunt and uncle I was happy. I forgot Paris—the school, the walls, the pavement. Especially when we visited the museum when it was closed. At those times, the dream was mine alone—all I had to do was look around me. I admired the paintings depicting battles at sea and ports devoted to commerce and piracy. I ran my fingers over ancient cast-iron cannons, wooden dinghies, and slender hempen cords. I circled the models of corvettes and sloops, cutters and seventy-four-gun ships; and I especially loved to imagine them casting off, unfurling their sails, and heading out to sea with their crews. I saw straight-backed men in blue and red uniforms standing on the forecastles of sailing ships, and agile, brawling sailors with scarves around their heads, climbing barefoot up the rigging. I heard the snapping of the sails, the whistling of the southern wind, the violent roaring of the waves. I escaped reality. And when I emerged from my daydream, Uncle Jacques would take me over to the rope display and explain the use of each one, or else he would show me the instruments explorers used—sextants, octants, theodolites, and chronometers. It was sheer happiness.

One of these trips to the vast museum rooms remains

firmly engraved on my memory. Uncle Jacques had been ill and was having trouble walking, so he decided to tour the museum by bicycle! As he didn't want me running after him, he gave me permission to follow him on roller skates — a unique honor due to my age and our special relationship. What a show it must have been: Jacques Vichot on a bicycle, flanked by little Anne on her skates, sailing past all those glass display cases filled with the vestiges of the most prestigious ships in history. The museum guards were speechless.

But Uncle Jacques was not content simply to show me his museum, his life's work. He taught me how to look at the ocean with curiosity. Even more, he inspired me to regard it with a passion that was both physical and intellectual. Not only was the ocean a playground and a source of pleasure, it was a whole new universe, which, at the time, was no more understood than Jupiter or Mars. He spoke to me of mysterious tides, of incongruous examples, of microscopic marine organisms, of bottomless pits, of tricky currents, of trade winds and flying fish, of strange animals whose names I didn't know: killer whales, pilot whales, humpback whales, belugas.

Uncle Jacques was for me another Captain Ahab, another legendary sailor like Bernard Moitessier, with the all-important difference that I could see him every week, pester him, and wear him out with my questions. The first map of the ocean floor published by *National Geographic* hung on his wall. At the point when he felt I was truly interested, he took it down and gave it to me as a present. Today I realize this was only one of the many times that he paid me special attention, but the day he gave me that map — which I have piously preserved — Uncle Jacques did something extraordinary:

he gave me confidence in myself. He showed me an adult could care about a child's interests, could support and even encourage them.

Uncle Jacques was an example, a point of reference, an accomplice. It also turned out that he liked to shake things up. I remember one Sunday morning in Brittany when I was about ten years old. We were on vacation, and Uncle Jacques and Aunt Régine had come to pay us a visit. My uncle took me with him to Camaret to do some shopping, and we walked into the pastry shop. In and of itself, this was enough to surprise me. My mother did not like sweets, and we were permitted only one cake a year: a big mocha birthday cake, covered with crushed almonds. Four children, four cakes a year—no more.

That Sunday morning, without the least pretext of a birthday, Uncle Jacques announced his intention to buy everyone a chocolate cream puff! Not one big, collective, "reasonable" cake, but gourmand delicacies—individual, personal, egotistical. These were the kind of *choux à la crème* locally known as *religieuses*—literally translated, "nuns." A sin in all its splendor, and just when people were coming out of church!

While the girl counted out ten chocolate cream puffs, my uncle looked on with a little disappointed pout.

"What do you say, Anne?" he asked. "Don't you think they look a little skimpy?"

To my wondering eyes, it looked like she'd erected an entire mountain of cream. Of course, I didn't dare reply. My uncle continued in this same vein:

"We'll need at least two per person. Please, miss, make that twenty cream puffs."

For a split second, I thought that the walls of the pastry shop would crumble, that the heavens would open, that a flash of lightning would destroy the whole town of Camaret. Twenty chocolate cream puffs! It was more than audacious, it was begging for trouble. I still had not recovered from my stupefaction when Uncle Jacques added:

"To wrap things up, I'd like one more, but don't put it in with the others. I think my niece would enjoy eating it on the way home."

I left the pastry shop holding my gift like a choirboy carrying the Holy Communion. And then I bit into it, right there on the sidewalk, shivering with pleasure and delight. It was the best cream puff I have ever eaten! I remember the way Uncle Jacques looked at me, delighted and tender at the same time. And worried, too, because he probably thought I didn't dare rock the boat enough. He felt the dawning of an interest deep inside of me, which he still was at odds to understand, but that sometimes managed to express itself, especially when the subject of the ocean came up. He sensed that I was working against myself, getting through school by sheer discipline, with no goal in sight. That was the day that I think he leaned toward me and whispered in my ear:

"You shouldn't always do the reasonable thing. You've got to learn to do what you want, sometimes. Follow your heart, Anne."

I'm not really sure that he actually pronounced these words. But every time I remember the scene, I think I see him lean toward me, put his hand on my shoulder, and say these words in my ear, as if they were the key to the meaning of life. In any case, his gesture had the same significance.

Before vacation was over, I had decided to become an

oceanographer. Today, this term makes me smile. It is possible to become a physicist, a chemist, a biologist, a statistician, or a mathematician, or to choose a certain specialty in marine or earth sciences, but it is no more possible to become an "oceanographer" than to become an "earthographer." Why not a "planetologer"? Today, no one can seriously pretend to comprehend all the aspects of a subject as vast as the ocean. But in the 1960s, for a ten-year-old kid, it was still permissible. This was especially true because I still didn't know exactly what it was I wanted to do, except to follow Uncle Jacques's advice and never, ever again let anyone else decide for me how I should follow my heart.

When the films of Jacques Cousteau came out, they anchored me more deeply in my love of the sea and marine life, with its different kinds of flora and fauna. We didn't have a television set, so I racked my imagination figuring out how to show up at my friends' homes exactly in time to catch the episodes of his documentary. I didn't miss a single program. In my dreams, I was already a researcher. I paced the deck of my personal *Calypso* and dived down to tweak the fin of Jojo the grouper. I floated among the flotsam and jetsam of mysterious sea wrecks, or was the first to observe a giant deep-sea creature with a bristling jawful of razor-sharp teeth. Naturally, I escaped with a stroke of my flipper and named the beast straightaway, shamelessly calling it *Giganticus colletus*.

A few years later, I was going to high school at the Lycée Victor Duruy. This was another story altogether. Physics and chemistry bored me to tears, I was zero in French, and doing about average in biology, geography, and history. The only things that really interested me were art and math. Because I was quite undisciplined, the vice principal thought he would punish me by automatically assigning me to a branch of courses designed for humanities students. I probably would have accepted this decision, which would have opened the doors to art school, if I hadn't been possessed by a passion for the ocean. The chance to be rid of certain annoying subjects was quite tempting, but the very idea that a university science department could refuse my application sent cold chills running down my spine. At the beginning of the seventies, it still was inconceivable in France that anyone could become a researcher without first studying math. To follow the humanities at the lycée was to be barred entrance to the halls of science forever.

For me, such a refusal meant being cut off from the sea—and this was out of the question. "Follow your heart," Uncle Jacques had told me. And so I came to understand that skipping school was not necessarily the easiest route to satisfying those blasted desires of mine. I was going to have to work hard! I changed schools, enrolled in science courses, and plunged into my physics and chemistry books. I slogged away, keeping my blinders on in order to avoid distraction. And three years later, in June 1973, I graduated with the "right" diploma. Pocketing my pink acceptance form, I soon set off by train to Brest to enroll at the university in the department of marine biology.

The euphoria I felt about my new life didn't last long. During those first few months of study, I often cursed Uncle Jacques. Consult my own desires . . . follow my heart. First I had to know what I wanted to do, discover what I really loved. In general, my professors were intelligent, qualified, and interesting, but dredging up their students' hidden vocations was not part of their job. My fellow students were fairly friendly, but most of them didn't know what they wanted to do in life any more than I did. Only the ocean, so close at hand, attracted me, fulfilled me, and filled me with wonder.

I followed the coastline more assiduously than I ever attended classes. My minor subject was bird-watching, but I acted like an attentive amateur, nothing more. I majored in weekend parties at our house near Camaret. Since my family lived in Paris, I was the only student with a house all to herself. I covered hundreds of miles in sailboat races, and my friends and I founded the Crocodiles de l'Élorn, one of the first windsurfing groups in France. I also had to repeat my first year of college, just like Eric Hussenot, one of my oldest friends, who today is the co-director of Océanopolis in Brest.

I might well have repeated the year a third time and finally left the university disappointed, frustrated, and still undecided, but something happened to upset this round of fruitless study and perpetual extracurricular activity. One morning, on a beach near Cape Raz, a friend equipped me from head to toe: wet suit, weight belt, mask, flippers, and snorkel. He went into the water and invited me to follow. For days he had been promising me a surprise, all the while refusing to tell me anything about it.

"Now are you going to tell me what we're doing here?"

"Come and see. I'm sure you're going to like it."

It was impossible to get another word out of him. I either had to dump the equipment and leave him there, or follow him. I don't like guessing games, but I am a curious person. And so I took the plunge.

We were in a little bay, at high tide, where fishing boats were tied to moorings about thirty meters from shore. We swam out to the farthest boat, where my friend signaled me to stop. He took out his diving knife underwater and started striking the anchor chain. Had he gone completely nuts? As he still seemed to be in possession of his faculties, I thought he had arranged to meet other divers and was signaling our arrival by the noise. Was this all a joke he had concocted with our friends at school?

I was expecting his accomplices to arrive at any moment when a shadow appeared to my right. Surprised, I put my hand on my friend's shoulder to attract his attention. He looked in the direction of the shadow and signaled me up to the surface.

"It's him!" he cried.

"Him who?"

"Jean-Louis. Take a big breath. You're going to need it."

There was no way to get anything else out of him. He had already stuck his snorkel in his mouth and was taking a deep breath. Then he dived again.

I followed him as before, keeping my guard up. The shadow I had glimpsed seemed shaped like a fish and looked about the size of a man. We descended four or five meters with my friend leading the way, then remained at this depth thanks to the lead on our weight belts. Suddenly, the shadow reappeared. This time it was right in front of me. A simple spot at first, it rapidly grew larger. The water was not clear enough for me to distinguish what it was, but I immediately thought of a shark. For decades, any creature resembling a shark had been baptized "Jean-Louis" by the

local fishermen. They considered them dangerous predators, if not to humans, then to fish.

Before I had a chance to move, the shadow was upon us.
It was not a shark but a dolphin, and a big one — *Tursiops trun-catus*, almost three meters long! Never before had I had the
chance to see a bottlenose dolphin, alive and so close. He
made straight for my friend, then stopped abruptly, with
the point of his snout less than fifty centimeters from the
mask. I don't know what I would have done if he had
come toward me, but I don't think I would have fled. No
doubt I would have braved it out, simply because I couldn't
have been more surprised if an ostrich had passed through
my garden at Camaret.

On the other hand, the worry I had when I thought about
sharks completely disappeared as soon as I knew we were
dealing with a dolphin. Instinctively I felt I had nothing to
fear. At the time, little was known about cetaceans. If anyone had done a survey of the students in the marine biology
department, the majority would have said that dolphins were
found only in tropical waters. Certainly nobody thought they
lived off one of the chilliest points of the coast of Brittany.

I was frightened as I watched the dolphin make a pirou-
ette. Passing beneath us with a little dive, he followed it
with a tailspin, then came up behind us, turned around,
and stopped again. My friend and I were running out of air
and had to go back to the surface. I was sure the dolphin was
going to disappear, but instead he followed us up and began
to swim around us in circles. Jean-Louis was obviously less
surprised by me than I was by him, but his familiarity with
people had not lessened his curiosity. He showed no sign of

fear but nevertheless remained beyond our reach—even if we had wanted to, we would not have been able to touch him.

I don't know what kind of game he was playing in approaching, pulling back, then returning. Whenever he stopped moving, I could sense him looking through my mask in search of eye contact. Illustrators tend to represent dolphins with doelike eyes, but seen close-up, their eyes, encircled with wrinkled eyelids, look more like those of a puffy old drunk.

Jean-Louis's back was the color of gray-blue satin, and his lighter-colored belly had the look of the softest silk. Thanks to their skin, dolphins can swim quickly, in bursts as fast as thirty-five to forty kilometers an hour. According to the laws of thermodynamics, a dolphin's size, weight, shape, and muscular mass should not allow it to swim faster than twenty kilometers an hour, for water has a resistance eight times greater than air, but a dolphin has speed in its very skin. If you look at it under a microscope, it has a very particular structure: a smooth surface layer, both thin and elastic, and a supple second layer, formed of papilla and canals, which adapts itself to differing conditions. Much like a mattress with springs, this underlayer gives way or resists, varying according to the water pressure. Highly endowed with nerves, the dolphin's skin transmits sensations to the brain, which analyzes them and sends its orders back again to the millions of cells in the skin. This adapts itself in turn, as the dolphin slightly modifies the surface of its body, absorbing the turbulence that would otherwise slow it down.

I like trying to imagine what animals might feel when they're faced with a human being. I think about this when

I feed my cat and he looks at me with those eyes of his, full of gratitude and round as the eyes of a fried fish. As he purrs and rubs so gratifyingly against my calves, I think he must see me as a great hunter. Every day, I offer him a delectable sampling of prey. So from time to time, if he proudly brings home a lizard more dead than alive to show me that he, too, knows how to hunt, I am always careful never to look sad or disgusted, for these are reactions he could never understand.

I don't know what Jean-Louis was hoping for when he came to bid us hello—some amusement, perhaps. He seemed particularly interested in my diving watch, or maybe it was the noise it made. He stuck his lower jaw up against it and emitted a series of clicking noises. I think the gears inside it intrigued him. As my watch was also going tick-tock, maybe he thought it was my echolocation transmitter.

And then he suddenly got tired of passively contemplating his visitors and left. With six or seven flicks of his tail, he again became a far-off shadow and finally disappeared.

Those of us in the human world swam back to the nearest boat and climbed in. I needed to recover from my emotions. My friend was wearing a satisfied little smile. He asked me if the surprise was worth the trip, and I merely said yes. I don't think I ever revealed to him how thoroughly the encounter had shaken me. As soon as I felt a bit like myself again, I bombarded him with questions.

"How did you discover him?"

"Oh, I didn't find him, he found me. I was diving about a thousand meters from here, gathering samples of algae, when he came barreling toward me. At first I thought he was a shark."

"Is that why you called him Jean-Louis?"

"The local fishermen named him. I told them I'd seen a dolphin, and they said he was a regular in the area, that he'd been paying them visits for months. In fact, all any of them has to do is get in his boat and the dolphin shows up and starts swimming around in circles."

"Have you come back to see him often?"

"Five or six times over the past three months."

"And has he shown up every time?"

"Always. If he isn't here immediately, I just make a noise that carries underwater and he's here in a few minutes. He must never go too far away."

"Are you sure he's the same one?"

"Certain. You saw him: he has a lighter patch beneath his flipper, on the left. I always know him by that scar."

"Is he always alone?"

"I think so. No one has ever seen him with a pod of other dolphins. So tell me, did you like it?"

The word was too mild. I was in seventh heaven. My heart was still beating hard, and at the same time I felt as if the pieces of a puzzle were magically falling into place. Although I still felt confused, it was beginning to dawn on me why I had really come to Brest, and why I had begun a course of study that in many respects annoyed me to no end. What attracted me was the tremendous energy Jean-Louis gave off; to put it simply, it was the life force. My understanding of biology was etymological—literally, the study of life. Today, it still has the same meaning for me. The road to Brest was an obligatory route, one I had to travel to finally arrive on the path my heart wished me to follow.

It was not until much later that I understood this "Jean-Louis" who had moved me so deeply. To begin with,

Jean-Louis should have been called Jeanne-Louise, because "he" was a she. Second, my encounter had been with one of the solitary dolphins that are wrongly nicknamed "ambassadors" because they seem to appreciate the company of human beings. Far from acting as the "spokesmen" of their species, or the carriers of an obscure message, such individuals live excluded from their group. Whether this comes about through choice or rejection remains unknown.

Jean-Louis was amused by human incursions, as long as they remained rare and episodic, curious but respectful. As for me, I visited her fairly regularly for seven years, before some tactless person made the stupid and possibly money-grubbing move of advertising the presence of this exceptional creature. The success was astounding. Throngs of divers crowded Cape Raz. They came from everywhere— from all four corners of France, from Germany, Holland, and Spain. We saw as many as fifty at a time swimming in every direction, banging on pots and pans in the hope of attracting Jean-Louis for snapshots they would no doubt frame and deposit on their mantelpieces.

Jean-Louis let them have their way. And then, one day, she simply disappeared. Maybe she hid away in calmer waters or rejoined a group of other bottlenose dolphins. At least I hope so. Or maybe she died. When curious people mass together, others with weapons follow in their wake. On land and sea, life is menaced by trigger-happy people. Oh, the pleasure of shooting to score, of adding a new animal to the prize list! Too bad! This one's not on the list of endangered species! It's not even protected yet!

The dolphin wanted nothing except to be left in peace—

or at the least, to be left to decide on her own whether she wished to amuse herself in the company of two-footed creatures.

In my mind, this dolphin will always be a symbol of my future. It is not that this so-called ambassador transmitted a mission to me, but that she belongs to the experiences that helped me better to define what really matters in my life. "Follow your heart," as Uncle Jacques used to say. Whenever I listen to it, I always find the way to satisfy my needs. And if the wavelength is free of static, if I am sure I am on the path that's right for me, the obstacles disappear and every-thing becomes simple. But if I mistake my calling or lose my inner voice, I know I am in for a very rocky road.

Riding the Waves in Argentina

Here she comes! She's seen me! The whale's motions are imperceptible, and yet she is definitely moving. Giving the slightest wave of her tail, she propels her sixty tons in my direction, advancing with disconcerting ease. She's unused to seeing a minuscule human splashing about in the waters where she ritually comes to mate or give birth. She is intrigued. As for me, I've begun to wonder if I ever should have left the boat to take a swim with these giants. True, I did fly eight thousand kilometers over land and sea, traveling from France to Argentina for this rendezvous in the southern Atlantic with *Eubalaena australis*, the southern right whale, a close cousin of our northern right whale. But I had only come for purposes of research—not for a meeting face to face in the middle of the ocean with Leviathan.

Eight days earlier, I'd arrived with a small team of colleagues and nonprofessional naturalists at the airport in Trelew, in the region of Chubut, located in northern Patagonia. The trip had begun badly, as the contents of my suitcase had been stolen during a stopover in Brazil. All I had left was a thickly lined parka, the only loot the tropical thieves didn't know what to do with. I had hastily had to re-equip myself in Buenos Aires before taking off for the Atlantic coast.

In Trelew, we took a bus to the Valdès Peninsula and the village of Puerto Piràmides, which is located on the isthmus separating the Gulf of Nuevo to the south from the San José Gulf to the north. A few kilometers away, we found our hotel isolated in the pampas, a small former lighthouse that had been transformed into an *estancia*. It was both charming and glacial: there was no heat. The village, founded at the end of the nineteenth century to export wool and salt from Salina Grande, had neither dock nor pontoon, but proudly titled itself a "port." The absence of equipment did not bother the Argentineans, who were overflowing with imagination and gifted with rich and sometimes quite surprising ingenuity.

As the seabed of the Gulf of Nuevo ends in a gentle slope, the boat on which we had to embark could not approach the shore. Never fear—the sailors of Puerto Piràmides have invented the "rolling-floating pontoon." To the back of a tractor forgiving enough to hold up under re-peated exposure to seawater, they attached a sort of rolling scaffold put together with metal girders and rickety, mismatched wooden planks. They invited us to get up on this thing, prudently warning us to put on our life jackets first. As soon as we were on, squeezed together like sardines in a tin, the tractor driver started up this bizarre contraption and backed right up into the ocean! Almost immediately, the waves began to break against our refuge, soaking us from head to foot. When the tractor's wheels were halfway over the hub, our boat came up to the platform, permitting us to embark. On board, we were greeted by a smiling sixty-year-old captain with eyes like burning coals, silver hair, and deeply tanned skin—the image of a Patagonian god. The very incarnation of the Macho of the Pampas, he was straight out of a novel by Francisco Coloane. Of course, all of the women immediately fell for him.

As soon as our launch, propelled by two powerful outboard motors, headed out to sea, I forgot our impromptu bath on the pontoon and even the captain's smile. The whales were there to meet us, although we had come unannounced. There they were, only a few miles from shore, swimming to and fro in their mating grounds. Here, throughout the Southern spring (our Northern autumn), the whales give themselves over to a gargantuan ballet of love. This has been described by my colleague Roger Payne, the great specialist of southern right whales, who has made the Argentinean coast his special subject of study. He has acquired such an extraordinary amount of knowledge through long-term research in the region that he is able to identify every migrating whale arriving at the Valdès Peninsula after feeding for a season in the reaches of the Antarctic, beyond the southernmost tip of South America.

Right whales migrate five thousand kilometers in just a few weeks. The females are the first to arrive in the temperate waters. Shallow coastal seas, twenty to forty meters deep, seem most suitable for mating. The males, close behind, manifest their excitement by rolling in the water, striking the surface with their large, paddle-shaped flippers. At sea, the sound travels more than a kilometer.

The southern right whale conforms to the rule of safety in numbers in order to assure the survival of the species.

The males are here with one idea in mind: to mate as often
as possible with every female they can manage to mount.
They approach a female in a group and battle each other to
possess her. They shove and knock each other about, pushing with their foreheads and tearing their fragile skin.

Sometimes as many as six or seven males surround a
single female, who does not give herself up easily. Once they
catch up with her, she rolls over on her back and floats, her
belly in the air, keeping her genitals safe from the assault of
her would-be lovers' frightening pink penises. Ordinarily,
the male organ is concealed in a slot like a kind of zipper—
hydrodynamics *oblige*. Their testicles, like those of an elephant, are not visible, but remain in the interior of the
abdominal cavity, tucked beneath the kidneys. The penis,
made of fibrous matter, is kept in a protective sheath by
muscles shaped like a strap. The elasticity of this muscle
contributes to enormous erections: their penises can get
as long as two meters.

When the males surround a female and attempt to turn
her over, they transform the sea around them into a frothing
cauldron. Immense flippers, enormous heads covered with
callosities, and beating tails emerge from the waves. The female resists, but sooner or later she has to breathe—while
she floats on her back, her spout is submerged. And so she
rolls over and her suitors all rush in at once to get what
they've come for. The males are so ardent that sometimes
two of them simultaneously penetrate a single female.

As we entered the Gulf of Nuevo, the seas were still
calm. Often, the first thing we saw of the whales was their
tail flukes, enormous expanses four meters wide. For this

species of whale has the curious habit of "hanging" suspended in the water, head down, tail up. It is as if they use
their tail flukes as natural sails, going with the wind or just
letting themselves drift. Or maybe they are scouring the sea
floor. In truth, we know little or nothing about it.

Every time we watched them turn over and remount to
the surface to breathe, blowing their jet of vapor, their cor-
pulence surprised us. With its cousin from the far north, the
southern right whale is the most thickset of all the whales.
Devoid of a dorsal fin, its body is shaped like a barrel. It's a
colossus all right—heavy, slow, and somber, but with phenomenal strength. In whaling days, a harpooned animal
could drag a whaling ship around for over ten hours, even
with all its sails unfurled as a break. Whales such as these
were not called *right* because of their force of character, but
because they possessed a quality they could have done better without: once they were harpooned and slaughtered,
their cadavers did not sink. This was an invaluable stroke of
luck for whale hunters, a veritable floating fortune. The *right*
whale—the one that whalers thought was the best kill—ren-
dered enormous quantities of oil, and its huge baleen plates,
over two meters long and the silkiest of all, brought very
high profits when the ships came into port.

Along the Argentinean coast, during the first half of the
nineteenth century, the whalers from Nantucket and New
Bedford who inspired Herman Melville to write *Moby Dick*
killed eighteen thousand southern right whales. First they
harpooned the calves, thus guaranteeing that the females
would stay close to the boats, and then they took care of the
females. Year after year it was the same place, the same long

massacre. They didn't even have to search them out: the whales came on their own, like animals to the slaughterhouse. If the hunt had not already been cut back before it was finally outlawed, the species would have become extinct. Today their numbers fortunately seem to be on the rise again.

For six days, we went to meet the whales every morning. In the sort of expedition where embarking depends on an asthmatic tractor, the most difficult task was actually getting out to sea. After that, we headed off straight through the bay. We cut our motors as soon as we spied a female and her young, while we were still two or three hundred meters away. We only had to wait for the curious calf to approach to observe them at our leisure from the deck. Often, the calf rolls over on its side the better to observe its unknown visitors, or tries to push the boat with the tip of its snout. The mother watches warily, swimming in circles around the launch. Finally, when she judges that the game has gone on long enough, she intervenes, placing herself between the boat and her young, and gradually leads it away.

The first time I made this trip, cetaceans (the order of whales and dolphins) were not yet attracting large crowds and a boat was still a rare occurrence. The whales were not yet weary of human curiosity. The same scenario could be repeated five or six times a day. Today, ten years later, the rage for whale watching brings tourists by the droves to Mexico, Saint-Laurent, and the Argentinean coast. The skippers will do anything to satisfy their clients, and competition drives them to excess. They must get close to the animals—very close, as close as possible. Tired of being bothered and harassed, the whales finally end up leaving.

And when they are surrounded by five or six outboards at once, some of them start to get aggressive.

Ours were not, and we went about our work without a problem. I even tried to record their songs, as my hydrophone had escaped being pillaged by the baggage bandits. The equipment worked well: I captured the noise of our motors to perfection, but the divas turned out to be capricious. For six days running, they did not emit the least "audible" sound. No cries, no sighs. I think it was the silence on the end of the line that caused me to vary from my program for a few hours. Watching the same whales day after day from the deck of the launch as they became increasingly familiar made me want to swim among them. Today, the authorities prohibit diving, and fortunately so, because there are far too many people, and people in crowds often act stupidly. Back then, it was not exactly authorized, either. Let's just say it was tolerated—as long as it was done with discretion.

We left at dawn on the eighth day, driving a rattletrap 4x4, with our Zodiac, an inflatable dinghy, hitched on the trailer. Two of my companions undertook the adventure with me. Although they were not professional scientists— one was a banker and the other the director of a large company—they both respected animals, and I knew they were seasoned divers. It took us three hours to reach the beach where we wanted to launch the boat, a two-hour drive along a rutted trail studded with potholes, and a one-hour pit stop to repair a leaky tire at a gas station lost in the wilds of the pampas. It was the kind of place where you could be sure to see sheep, guanacos, and maybe armadillos. But human beings were few and far between, and those who had cars were even rarer.

I don't remember if the station actually sold gas, but I will never forget the looks of alarm we got from the local populace. We must have seemed like creatures from outer space as we got out of the car: we had donned our neoprene wet suits before leaving Puerto Piràmides, to avoid undressing on the windy, barren coast. True, we hadn't yet put on our flippers, but we looked ridiculous nonetheless. To try to recover our dignity a little, we firmly marched into the station while José, our guide, driver, and Zodiac pilot, repaired the defective tire. We even played miniature football—in our diving suits! Meanwhile, a pack of scraggly sheepdogs kept circling round us, sniffing at our calves and looking worried.

It is 10:00 A.M. when, one by one, we slide from the dinghy into the brisk water of the bay. Two hundred meters away, the whale I hope to approach seems motionless. I wonder how she will react when she senses our presence. Will she even see us? The answer is soon to come.

She sees me and begins to head my way. In a few seconds, she has reduced the distance between us by half. Another hundred meters and she will be on top of us. Not far to go. I feel my throat constrict and extend my arms to stabilize myself on the surface of the water. My wet suit buoys me up, and the light ballast at my belt allows me to float without difficulty. The current is weak and the waves negligible, the heavy swells of the open sea breaking at Punta Delgada, at the far end of the peninsula. All is calm and silent. My head above water, looking through my mask, I observe the black mountain slowly coming toward me.

I suddenly realize that I have been waiting for this moment unconsciously for years. Despite all the years I've spent studying cetaceans, at this instant I have no idea if I am about to realize my fondest dreams or pay the price of my folly. The water is thirteen degrees Celsius, but I doubt that I am trembling because of the cold. An interior voice tells me there is no danger, that this gigantic marvel cannot feel menaced by a bizarre little thing like myself, a thousand times smaller than she is. If she feared me, she would go away. Since she is approaching, she is not afraid. My interior voice draws certainty from experience: right whales do not attack, they do not devour people. Jonah is a myth. As for Moby Dick, he was a sperm whale, not a right whale. My voice keeps telling me this, but it is so small it can barely make itself heard over the beating of my heart. The whale is still getting closer, and I realize she has altered her path to a curve.

I turn toward my two companions, positioned some distance away, and repeat the advice I've already given them: "Make no sudden movements, and stick together. She must have no trouble seeing all three of us at once; above all, she must not think she is surrounded. Animals detest that. As long as she feels safe, we have nothing to fear." I don't know if I managed to persuade them; it was hard enough to convince myself.

Observing them from ship deck during research expeditions from the Arctic to the Antarctic, I had never doubted that baleen whales (the suborder of toothless cetaceans to which right whales belong) were peaceful creatures. Seen from above, that's obvious. In the water, it looks quite different.

In range of a tail four meters wide, whose merest flick is powerful enough to snap a boat in two, certitudes crumble. And what if she opened her immense mouth with those bucketlike jaws, as she does to gather food, filtering between her long baleen plates enormous quantities of water full of copepods, the tiny shellfish she's so wild about?

The whale swims around us three times, narrowing the circle each time in passing. I am certain she is a female; males do not come in so close to shore. Suddenly, she stops in front of me. She is twenty meters away, no farther. I contemplate her, forcing myself to remain calm. I have no idea if I'll live to remember this experience one day.

And then she rolls over on her side! Her formidable front flipper pointing straight toward the sky, the whale shows me her back—and continues to rotate. This time, I don't move a muscle. She has decided to approach by rolling over. It is like watching a semitrailer truck do somersaults in slow motion. Or worse, a deep-sea steamroller fifteen meters long. Even if I wanted to escape, I wouldn't have time. She rolls, and rolls again, every turn revealing a large white patch on her belly. Two more rotations, and she'll be on top of me. I instinctively hold my breath, my eyes fixed on that gigantic flipper rising and falling like the blade of a paddle wheel two meters long, and a good meter wide. For an instant, I think it is going to hit me and knock me cold. But no, it touches down on the surface of the water, just a few meters from my shoulder. I'm barely splashed. Of course, I am aware that she can calculate to the fraction of a millimeter how to position her forelimbs. Humans in the water lack a sense of distance, and their movements lose their precision. But whales are in their element and know how to take its measure. If she had wanted to brush up against me, she would have been as gentle as a mother's fingertips caressing a baby's cheek.

The whale stops, and I can clearly see the bonnet of callosities, the refuge of specialized crustaceans, decorating her forehead. It is the unique shape of this rough cushion that permits Roger Payne and his team to distinguish, identify, and keep track of individual whales. No doubt this one has a name, or at least an identification number.

She is so close I could reach out and touch her, but I keep myself from doing it. I am the intruder here. If we are to have contact, she must take the initiative. Like a Cyclops, she observes me out of one eye, the size of a big saucer. A thick "eyebrow" of callosities arches above it. The other eye looks out to sea on the opposite side of her enormous head, whose strongly curving, interminable mouth gives her the expression of a bulldog. She closes her eyelid, reopens it. Her gaze is hypnotic, nothing like that of a fish. If I still needed proof that the animal before me was a mammal, this one look would suffice. This similarity to our own species is what made me drop ornithology at the beginning of the 1970s and decide to study cetaceans.

The moment she looks me deep in the eye, I lose my apprehension. When she begins moving again, I immediately dive to watch her swim. Her black body threads smoothly by me, as if drawn by an invisible cable. She moves so quickly that I can only follow her for a few seconds. This time, I succeed in glimpsing the slight motion of her tail that suffices to propel her hydrodynamically perfect mass. A few seconds later she is already far away. I mount to the surface, spit out my mouthpiece to gulp a big breath of air, and rejoin my two companions, who are already back in the dinghy. I remain in the water, holding onto the side of the boat. I've hardly taken off my mask before they bombard me with questions.

"Did she touch you?" "Why was she rolling over like that?" "How come she came so close?"

They address me using the familiar "tu" for the first time. Social conventions break down when you take a bath with a whale in the South Atlantic, fifteen hundred kilometers from Buenos Aires. Treading water, I answer their questions, trying to remain as scientific as possible, enumerating the morphological characteristics of the baleen whale: the size of its baleen plates, two meters long; the shape of its tail flukes; the callosities on its forehead and jaws.

One of them asks why I didn't reach out my hand. I respond that I never take the initiative of touching animals, even if I have verified that cetaceans in captivity like to be petted—especially on the head or on the tongue. This is the case for certain killer whales, which faint with pleasure if you're brave enough to tickle them! But in the presence of wild animals at liberty in nature, I leave it to them to make the first move. From respect, first of all, but also because contact with a cetacean is never innocuous. Their sense of touch is different from ours. Their skin is soft and fragile; older animals bear innumerable scars from the wounds and scrapes they've received over the years.

The touch of a dolphin's wet skin is like the sensation of the finest silk. But if its skin remains in contact with the air for too long, it rapidly dries out and cracks. These cruel wounds inflict atrocious suffering. Whenever we transport ill or wounded animals, it is necessary to bathe them constantly with water, or to rub their skin with balm or Vaseline. Their highly specialized skin is devoid of keratin, a protein that protects but also lessens the subtlety of tactile sensation. Their skin also integrates an elaborate system of sensitive nerve endings, which are more abundant on certain parts of their bodies, and around the blowhole in particular. Whales cannot "see" whether they are immersed or not, because their blowholes are situated at the top of their skulls. It is thus their skin, greatly sensitized around their "nostrils," that informs them of their position. This picks up variations in localized pressure and indicates to the whale whether it is about to surface or not. Jaws are another sensitive region: dolphins (which belong to the suborder of tooth whales) use them to explore unknown objects that incite their curiosity. In addition, touching with their mandibles permits them directly to receive the echo of the high-frequency "clicks" they emit in order to obtain extremely precise information on the nature of the object.

Research has shown that the ability of their dermis to register variations in pressure plays an essential role in the speed cetaceans can attain. Wavelike microdeformations of their specially structured skins absorb the turbulence caused when they swim. When an animal advances rapidly, streams of water detach and bubble up around its body, increasing resistance and thereby breaking its speed. But the minuscule "waves" that run through a dolphin's skin, like the waves left in the sand when the water retracts, allow it to avoid the formation of such turbulence. Instead, water droplets "slide" along the animal's flanks, or rather the dolphin thereby manages to slip through the water, minimizing the effect of friction.

For a few minutes, my companions and I continue to exchange impressions.

"It's crazy how she's not even afraid of us."

"Why should she be afraid? No predator would dare attack her."

"All the same, they've been hunted for centuries. Even here, only a few miles from the open sea. I see how they could have been massacred so easily."

Admiring exclamations follow: "marvelous," "fabulous," "sublime," "indescribable," "unforgettable." Yet deep inside, as if I still have to persuade myself that what I have just experienced is really real, I keep repeating the same thing over and over: "I did it! I went swimming with the whale! It's terrific!" I'm in heaven, and it must show on my face. I have no desire to get back in the boat. I have the feeling it will really be over once I'm no longer in the water, and I am trying to prolong the emotion. All of a sudden, José points out to sea.

"*Mira!* Look! She's coming back! She's coming back!"

And he's right. After drawing back, the whale had made a half turn to take another look at these strange visitors. When she was no farther than forty or so meters behind the dinghy, she turned and "lay down" on her left flank, the better to see us once she came up level with the boat. In this position, her front flipper was pressed against the length of her side, while one of her tail flukes rose up from the surface of the water, over a meter high. José clutched the handle of the outboard motor while my companions huddled on the bottom of the boat.

"*Cuidado,* Anne, she's coming straight for you!"

I see her coming but am not afraid. In any case there is nothing I can do to get out of her way, and I'll do nothing to frighten her. I only bend my knees, so she needn't plunge too deeply. Most of all, I want to see her close up, one more time. She passes beneath me slowly, eyeing our white rubber dinghy, which she easily could use as a beach ball, just two meters away. Southern right whales have often been observed playing with floating objects. Most of the time, they push them with their muzzles. This one seems not to be in a humorous mood, but contents herself with gliding by, very slowly. . . .

All of a sudden, I understand what is about to happen and a shiver runs through my body. The whale has remained on her flank, the better to observe us with her lateral eye, the great black triangle of her tail fluke still sticking out of the water. She advances, without seeking to avoid me. Instinctively, I let go of the dinghy and spread my legs as far as possible, so the hard rubber of my old flippers won't scrape her sides. Suddenly her tail fluke is up against my back, and I am carried off for a dozen meters, riding on the back of Leviathan! I weigh no more than a feather on her back, but she feels me, pivots in full course, and begins a slow dive. Taking care not to hurt me, she leaves me at the surface and disappears.

Ten seconds. It lasted only ten tiny seconds, but they remain engraved on my mind as one of the most beautiful memories of my life, and one of the most moving experiences of my entire career.

Once I'm back on the dinghy after my ride, my companions observe me in silence. It's as if I had come from another planet, my face marked with strange stigmata. No doubt I was simply wearing the blissful smile of a happy child. I sit in the bottom of the boat, José pulls hard on the starter, and the outboard roars. As we head off into the distance, commentary would be superfluous. We are in a hurry, for that section of the coast is classed as a natural reserve, and our authorization has run out.

After we've gone for about a mile, one of my companions cries out:

"There she is again! She's spouting!"

She had just emerged in a cloud of mist. She was swimming a hundred meters away, keeping her trajectory parallel with ours. As a scientist, I naturally require a certain rigor of myself when it comes to interpreting animal behavior, but that day, frankly, I had no idea what was going on in that whale's head. For the sake of a good story, I am pleased to think that she insisted on accompanying us because she understood we were leaving. She even seemed to want to leave us with a yet more impressive memory. Deciding to dive, she disappeared for a few seconds. Then, suddenly, her head broke the surface, and she leapt entirely out of the water in an impressive arc before falling back again on her flank, making an enormous splash. A leap of formidable power.

All of us, including José, cried out in a chorus of admiration. It was a breathtaking spectacle. When the wave she made reached us, our rubber dinghy danced like a cork. We

hardly had time to grab hold of the sides to try to regain
our balance when the whale began again. A second breach,
just like the first. And then a third, and a fourth. Adjusting
her speed to ours, she leapt, each time level with the boat,
keeping a respectable distance so we would not interpret her
game as a gesture of intimidation. We shrieked with joy like
children at a show of fireworks.

"Five! Six! Seven! Eight! Nine! Again! And again!"

All in all, we counted twelve. Twelve successive breaches,
each as powerful as the next, all beautiful enough to make
you cry. Extravagant, majestic salutes, the unforgettable good-
bye of a giant. I think I had tears in my eyes: I had felt so
many emotions in a single hour.

Once we were back on shore, we loaded the dinghy back
on the trailer and returned to Puerto Piràmides. We told
our adventure to the rest of the team, but I don't think we
were really able to communicate the emotion of it. Maybe it
is indescribable. And yet I know our encounter left no one
there untouched. For my companions as well as for myself,
the salutary image of this nearly invulnerable creature, so
powerful and yet so totally serene, surely remains an unforgettable memory. I keep this image with me as a radical cure
for monotony, guarding it preciously like an interior flame
to illuminate my research through days that are often tedious
and repetitive, or even, at times, discouraging.

I did not experience my ride on the whale's back as some
kind of mystical "contact." I don't believe that whales and
dolphins are sacred. Such worship comes from ignorance
or, worse, stupidity. And it sometimes stems from a deliber-
ate policy whose goal is blatantly political or commercial.

Furthermore, I have too much respect for animals to find any interest in pursuing them like a thrill collector. My ambition goes beyond simply following cetaceans as they migrate around the world and diving here and there in their stopping places. My responsibilities as a professional scientist consist first in understanding them and, if necessary, in defending them in case they are really in danger. This is not always simple to evaluate. I know I will pass ten or even a hundred times more hours at my computer or my microscope than in the bays of the South Atlantic.

That said, if my whale so wished it, I would voluntarily return tomorrow, with my mind completely at rest, for no other reason than the pleasure of it. My bags are packed. I am ready for another waltz, because the first one was troubling, spontaneous, intense, and deeply pleasing. That whale gave me energy, and continues to do so, like all the animals I've come to know over the course of my travels—timid seals on the Magdalen Islands, a lost walrus at Saint-Palais-sur-Mer, an ill-tempered sperm whale in the Bay of Biscay, an easily spooked arctic narwhal, lecherous elephant seals on the Argentinean coast, insolent swallows in Patagonia, an irascible fur seal in a crater on Deception Island, and many more. They live within me and encourage me to keep on going, just as surely as any of the exceptional people I have had the good fortune to encounter—obsessive tuna fishermen from Vigo, Cambridge academics who love their pints of beer, Polish sailors cast away on Spitsbergen, rescuers of orcas in the Kerguelen Islands, or children filled with wonder on the *Fleur de Lampaul*.

Our world is unbelievably beautiful and alive. I will

never tire of observing it, nor will I ever cease to be moved by a sublime landscape, the texture of a rock, and the power of the elements that formed them. I will always be filled with wonder at the magic of lightning, the delicacy of tiny flowers, glowing lichens, curious animals, and fascinating people. This beauty nourishes me, and it is more important as a source of energy than any of the delicious food I eat. And Lord knows I do love to eat!

This is my good fortune: after ten long hours at the microscope, or three days spent in a meeting to arrive at a consensus that should have taken two hours, or whenever else I start to doubt I have chosen the path that is right for me, life itself always comes to my rescue.

Hundreds of Thousands of Dolphins . . . and Their Ghosts

Perched on the crosstrees seven meters above the deck, I looked down into the Bay of Biscay. All around the sailboat as far as I could see, the ocean was seething, bubbling with effervescence. There was not a breath of wind, yet the surface was covered with whitecaps, as if it were swept by violent gusts coming from opposite directions. Hundreds of fins, shining in the early morning light, were simultaneously breaking the surface every second. Dolphins! Tens of thousands of dolphins, as far as the eye could see. I was right in the middle of one of the largest aggregations ever observed at high sea off the coast of France. Never before had I witnessed such a spectacle, and I knew I would probably never see it again. It was simply beyond imagination.

Half an hour earlier, I had dragged myself out of the mess room, clutching my toothbrush, to join the crew on watch in the cockpit. I was shivering despite two sweaters and my watchman's jacket. The air was very brisk, and I had wrongly predicted that it was going to be a bad day. There was barely a swell, the wind was low, the waves were lapping quietly, the sky was the color of lead, everything was gray. It was a classic case of the anticyclonic conditions typical of

May, which had the further distinction of putting our skipper in a very foul mood. We'd been at sea for thirty-some
hours, going along at a lamentable three knots on a sailboat
designed for racing, a thoroughbred half-tonner reputed to
test the mettle of its crew at the lightest hint of a breeze.

We'd shipped out from Brest the night before, hoping to
enter the Straits of Antioch by early afternoon. Now, if the
calm persisted, chances were that we wouldn't make dock
until the middle of the following night. This would give us
only a few hours' sleep before setting out on the first regatta
early the following morning.

In 1977, the races of La Rochelle Week occurred in late
spring, taking place without interruption from Ascension
weekend through Pentecost. It was ceaseless competition and
one long party, even if the time of heroic binges—half on the
water, half in the bars—was finally coming to an end. The future would belong to strictly professional sportsmen, early-
to-bed types with a tendency to take themselves a bit too
seriously. For us, exams were just around the corner. We were
set on getting drunk on sea spray before exchanging our card
tables for benches in the exam room and our hangovers for
study headaches.

I was about to go back down to make coffee and wake
my three teammates when the skipper called out grouchily,
"Hey, we've got dolphins."

The group he had spotted was off the bow of the ship,
veering to starboard. There were six of them, each about
two meters long. I could tell they were common dolphins
from the coloration of their black backs and gray and ocher
flanks. Swimming at full speed, they crossed our path at a
forty-five-degree angle.

This was not my first encounter at sea, but over the past few months I'd felt a dawning interest in cetaceans. With a handful of friends from the marine biology department, I'd got into the habit of going up and down the Brittany headlands to observe the marine mammals found along the coast. We tried to approach the seals, and on several occasions had already found dolphins washed up on the beaches. When I attempted to find information to improve our observations, I realized very little was known about the subject. So little, in fact, that, ignorant as we were, our dilettantish studies could still be quite useful.

"Look, there are more of them to port side."

I wheeled around to discover two other groups of the same species, but in even larger numbers. There were about fifteen adults, adolescents, and calves.

"There are more behind us, too . . . and in front!"

Intrigued at first, I quickly felt a strange, almost troubling, sense of some abnormal presence. I left the cockpit and went to the forecastle. Three striped dolphins, their slender bodies streaked with a flame of white, were trying to surf the wave at our stem, but we were going too slowly to keep them amused for long. I went to the boom, where I observed a dozen or so groups of common and striped dolphins mixed together.

Then I decided to climb the mast in order to get some height. Someone handed me the boatswain's slatted chair, used to repair problems in the masts if hardware breaks or a halyard jams. The chair is always kept at hand in a trunk in the cockpit. I sat down in it and attached the harness to a halyard. My teammates wound the other end of the rope around a winch and hoisted me like a sail all the way up to my perch on the crosstrees. And then the first dolphins leapt out of the water: wave on wave of bounding animals, stretching out to infinity.

The sight of them left me dumbstruck. Where were they coming from? Where were they going? Why were they massing together? At the time, we knew only that dolphins were usually observed in small pods much like family units, rather than always living in large schools. Although they belong to the suborder of tooth whales, dolphins are not migratory animals like other whales, which are genetically programmed to follow certain routes and arrive year after year at the same time, in the same well-defined territory, to feed or reproduce. This leaping horde thus was not the aquatic equivalent of a flight of storks or an interminable procession of African gnus. Later, my observations and others I collected from fishermen and vacationers helped me to understand the nature of dolphin displacement throughout the northeast Atlantic.

It was more akin to nomadism than mass exodus. Even if the displacement of large populations lacks the regularity of migration, I was nonetheless able to trace a seasonal pattern of movement from the southeast toward the northwest. The dolphins leave the Bay of Biscay in the spring to meet up in the Celtic Sea at the edge of the continental shelf. This is a zone where the ocean abruptly deepens, and fish at that season abound. Dolphins are predators that follow their prey, and they long ago established a "map of easy pickings" when it comes to seasonal fishing for sardines or horse mackerels. In winter, they come back to the Bay of Biscay. In 1977 none of this was known yet, and the subject had fascinated me for so long that I felt I just had to learn to understand it.

Four years later, I explained it in my doctoral thesis on the
biology and reproduction of the common dolphin.

But perched in the crosstrees, I was shaken to the core
of my being. There was something supernatural in the spectacle before me, like the experience of an aurora borealis or
a volcanic eruption. Marvelous or tragic, such occasions
universally serve as crucibles for the imagination. The gathering was so dense that I no longer knew if the water was
bearing the dolphins, or if they were engendering the sea.
It released a mysterious, fundamental energy, a wild, inspira-
tional beauty of which legends are born. This Dionysiac
bubbling up awakened memories of the mythology that
had enchanted me as a child: the myth of the giant dolphin,
womb of the world, who was really Apollo disguised to fool
humans; the torture of St. Lucian of Antioch, whose cadaver,
thrown to the monsters of the sea, was brought back to shore
by a school of dolphins so he could have a decent burial. I
truly believed the dolphin fresco at the palace at Knossos in
Crete had come to life before my very eyes. I thought about
the mutinous sailors from ancient Greece who were transformed into dolphins by the god of the abyss to draw his
chariot of seashells. In a fraction of a second, one of nature's wonders can awaken three thousand years of myth.

And, more modestly, change the direction of an entire
life.

∾

Twenty years later, the winter of 1996–97. At the Center
for Research on Marine Mammals in La Rochelle, which I
founded and have directed since 1995, the telephone rings
at the break of dawn, and all activity abruptly halts. We all

prick up our ears in the offices, as Isabelle, our assistant, answers the phone. We all are hoping against hope that it won't be bad news.

"Yes, sir, this is the place. Where are you calling from? Where exactly did you see them? How many were there? Six, you said? We're coming, sir. Thank you for notifying us."

A disappointed hope—it's another stranding. My colleagues are already hard at work. They didn't even stop at the Center this morning before hitting the road. By dawn, they were on the beach at Landes, Gironde, Charente-Maritime, Vendée, or Loire-Atlantique. Once again today, there's no escaping it. I don't even feel apprehension anymore—no anger, no sadness. I only feel more heartsick than I've ever felt in my life. I'm also worn out from the fatigue of driving five hundred or six hundred kilometers every day now for two full weeks, including weekends. The thought of giving up crosses my mind only for a split second. I cannot let down the network of volunteers who help us all year long without a thought to the amount of time they give. I don't have the right. They are waiting for me to take action, and that's just what I'm going to do.

There is nothing to do but grab a dissection kit, throw my boots, gloves, and slicker into the car, and take off in the pouring rain to some remote beach, gritting my teeth. I know what's waiting for me: six cadavers in a more or less advanced state of decomposition. I might not even be able to determine the species. Most likely their tails will have been amputated, or I'll have to sever a nylon rope knotted around the stem of their tails, encrusted into their flesh. This is the road to horror.

It's the beginning of March. We received the first call about a dead specimen on February 13, and the telephone has not stopped ringing since. In twenty days, we have counted the cadavers of 629 dolphins, washed ashore on the Atlantic littoral running from Bayonne to Brest. A few weeks later, they would number over 700. In one week alone, the guard from the Arguin reef, driving up and down the beaches in his 4x4, located seventy dead animals—common dolphins, striped dolphins, pilot whales, and even some extremely rare porpoises. A retired couple on Oléron Island, faithful correspondents of the Center, discovered fifty cadavers—more dolphins than they had ever seen in their lives. There were two dead whales as well, including a fin whale calf, tangled up in the remains of a fishing net. Hundreds of animals, trapped, asphyxiated, mutilated, then thrown away like garbage. Already in 1989 we had discovered hundreds of victims. But this time it was wholesale slaughter. Or rather, the ocean had revealed a tiny fraction of the general massacre.

Every winter from February to March, and sometimes for a longer period from January to April, the sea deposits the cadavers of dolphins along the Atlantic coast. We ended up by calling it "stranding season." Throughout these months, one low-pressure system follows another, all of them coming from the west. It begins with winds from the southwest that first head east, then northeast, under a heavy sky. These winds create a powerful swell, pushing anything that floats toward the shores of France: torn-up algae, old fishing nets, driftwood, assorted garbage, and cargo fallen from freighters. This is how the waves sometimes

wash up hundreds of tennis shoes, paint cans, or even deto-
nators for explosives! If the storms are farther out to sea, or
if they are shorter and less frequent, the beaches are far less
littered with detritus. On the other hand, if the low-pressure
systems follow one another for weeks on end, and especially
if they coincide with periods of extreme tides, then the
"spoils" can be outstanding. This is because of the persis-
tent swell, and above all because the currents then are powerful enough to lift dead animals weighing a hundred kilos
from the bottom of the ocean and push them toward the
shore.

Examining cadavers along the coast, I've seen stones
weighing from twenty to thirty kilos washed up on the
beach. Laminaria, seaweed that grows some ten meters
down, was still clinging to them. The current had torn them
up from the bottom, and probably carried them for several
kilometers before tossing them at our feet. These natural
phenomena explain why we had been inundated with dolphins that winter. They did not cause the deaths; they only
revealed the exceptionally high death rate by washing the
cadavers to the shore. Human beings were the sole culprits.
All these animals were victims of human negligence and
stupidity, of the human "genius" for inventing the worst
and believing we've created the best.

Try to imagine a pelagic trawl: an immense funnel more
than four hundred meters wide and nine hundred meters
deep. A veritable abyss! At the same time, imagine this funnel
simultaneously dragged along by two ships like oxen before a
plow, for a single trawler powerful enough to pull this gigantic hoop does not exist. The pelagic trawl is far more devastating than the drift nets that are so often condemned, and

sometimes prohibited, but that obviously cause less damage. In terms of arms, the drift net is a light rifle; the pelagic trawl is a heavy machine gun. In the hands of a dolt, the rifle can be deadly, but it remains selective. But a machine gun, even when it is handled by an expert, makes no distinctions. And neither does the pelagic trawl, which sucks in everything in its path.

Before pelagic trawling was invented, the classic trawl, which is much, much smaller, was dragged along either the surface or the bottom. From that point forward, the pillage could take place at any depth. Electronic detection devices installed on the ships pick up schools of fish, and the funnel is unfurled. But while fishermen are searching for hake or anchovies, the pelagic trawl sucks in everything, including species rarely caught in the past, like emperors or pomegranate fish, which live hundreds of meters down. These creatures look so unappetizing that they are sold with their heads off, as fillets. And in cases where the trawl rakes up anything and everything, mixing up all sorts of fish, the whole lot is dumped back into the sea, because no one on a factory ship has the time to sort them. The "useless" catch is tossed overboard as quickly as possible in order to redeploy the net as quickly as possible. Tons and tons of dead fish are thrown overboard—a monstrous waste.

But while the death of marine mammals still has the power to move public opinion, who is going to get excited about overfishing for hake and anchovies? Who will demonstrate to save herrings from extinction? And yet, if they disappear, their extinction will lead to that of their predators, the dolphins, which no longer will have anything to eat. And what will become of the fishermen themselves, once there is nothing left to fish? We can make a net as big as the Bay of Biscay, pulled by all the fishing boats on the whole Atlantic coast, but if the sea is empty, the net will be empty too. And then regret will set in—when it's too late.

The fishermen know this. They know the sea better than anyone. They may fear it at times, but they love it. They are not the ones responsible for this relentless pursuit, which, if it is not stopped, will end by wiping them out. They themselves are quite clear about this: "We know it's insane, but we keep doing it to earn money for our sons' educations, because we know they won't have anything to fish. The work's too hard. It's not the sea that scares us; it's this madness that makes us empty the ocean, all for a few dimes."

So who is responsible? It's you, it's me, it's all of us who don't want to pay, or cannot pay, for fish at higher prices. So we buy fish at $3.95 a pound, farm-raised fish, produced by intensive methods that pollute our bays and estuaries, just as intensive hog farming pollutes our rivers and groundwater. Or we eat fish that's been caught by pelagic trawling, bought from fishermen at barely seventy-five cents a pound and sold at the market for five times more: wholesalers, transporters, and fishmongers also have to earn a living.

And the owner of a fishing boat, too, had better be damn productive to make ends meet at the end of the month after paying the sailors and taking care of fuel, the loan on the boat, and other expenses. So he is tempted by the latest pelagic trawl, even bigger than the one before, especially since it is subsidized by the state or the European Union. He is told he must fish more, and more cheaply, in order to turn a profit. He follows the crowd and gets himself a monstrous piece of equipment to rake in the sea. In any case, if he doesn't do it, the next guy will—so goes the ultimate argument of those who try to exculpate themselves. I've met many fishermen who no longer like their profession, who feel uncomfortable, almost ashamed, of the methods. But how can they do otherwise? How can they hold out under pressure when the bank is calling in its loans? How can they not be tempted when fantastic subsidies are offered for the latest, state-of-the-art equipment? How can they stay afloat in the midst of fierce competition? How can they explain to housewives and supermarket managers that they must agree to pay higher prices for fish?

This is the reason that we, too, are responsible, from the simple consumer on up to the politician who makes the decisions, caught between pandering to a constituency on the one hand and avoiding the wrath of lobbyists on the other. How easy it is to accuse farmers of polluting the rivers when we've encouraged them for twenty years to cultivate their crops with pesticides and chemical fertilizers. How easy it is to point our fingers at the "bad" fishermen who exhaust stocks of fish and kill the "nice" dolphins when we reward them for relegating traditional boats to the junk heap and subsidize the cost of buying monstrous trawls. And when we've finally emptied the ocean through overfishing and pollution, whom will we accuse then? And what good will a scapegoat do us when it's too late to go back?

We're not there yet, but we're not far from it. For now, the mess stinks only of dead marine turtles and dolphins whose carcasses are piled up in garbage dumps all along the western coast of France from Saint-Gilles-Croix-de-Vie to Royan. Sometimes I think I spend more time on garbage heaps than on beaches. And once I'm there, the sight of

these animals—glorious yesterday, today rotten, half-
devoured, and thrown pell-mell in a heap—is terrifying. I
have to forge a mental shield in order not to cry, scream,
or vomit. Wading through, extracting teeth to determine
their age at death, taking organs from the least rotted specimens: it is necessary to master disgust and fury in order to
observe it all, note it all down, thank the volunteers, explain
to curious bystanders what has happened, and authorize
incineration when it is requested. And simply to continue
on with open eyes, because the spectacle is so abominable.

How many times as I returned from these mass graves,
driving like an automaton, have I imagined the torture these
animals must have endured. All along the coast in winter,
they're on the hunt for schools of fish, just like our fishermen. Whole schools of dolphins are taken at once—ten,
twenty, or thirty at a time, trapped in the pelagic trawl net
with their prey. They panic, unable to find the exit to the
hoop, and die a slow death. Breathing is not an involuntary
reflex for cetaceans; it is voluntary. Dolphins do not swallow water accidentally, and they do not drown, because they
know they mustn't breathe underwater. If they are caught in
a fishing net, they suffocate from lack of oxygen. When the
net is drawn up, the fishermen have no choice but to throw
this burdensome, inedible catch back into the sea, because
they are a protected species whose sale is forbidden. But an
adult dolphin weighs about a hundred kilos, and its slick
skin turns it into a slippery torpedo. So they tie a rope
around its tail, hoist it with a winch, then cut the rope and
dump it overboard. Or else they sever the tail, to save a
meter of nylon rope. Sometimes, they gut the animal so

it doesn't float to the surface after its entrails bloat with gas. This way, it can't be carried on the swell toward the coast, and no one will ever know how it died.

In the winter of 1996–97, in three-quarters of the cases where decomposition was not too far advanced to make reliable conclusions impossible, the animals we found on the beaches still wore signs of their capture: a rope cutting into their flesh, or their tails sliced clean off their bodies. I haven't the faintest doubt about the cause of the new "death rate" endangering dolphins off the coast of France, whose gravity has been revealed to us by a conjunction of meteorological forces. In the absence of a scientific statistical study, we can only estimate the size of the loss: without a doubt, five thousand to ten thousand dolphins, without distinction as to age or sex, die in pelagic trawls in the Bay of Biscay every year.

Every winter, we may be massacring as many dolphins as I was fortunate enough to see in a single glance. Writing this, I see them again, alive, superb, and free, bounding all around my sailboat, exactly as they were twenty years ago, almost to the day.

From Land to Sea

Imagine a wolf. A big wolf, almost the size of a bear, with an elongated muzzle and the mouth of a predator bristling with nasty teeth—razor-sharp incisors, fiercely pointed canines, and grinding molars. Its fur is perhaps rust-colored. It has a long tail, pointed ears, and a solid set of muscles. Now imagine this wolf hunting down its prey in a swamp, because that is where it finds the fish that have made up most of its diet for thousands of years. It advances, approaching without a sound, then leaps, plunging its muzzle into the muddy water to seize a squiggling fish between its powerful, pincerlike jaws.

This strange wolf, whose paws end in hooves, not toenails, is a mesonychid, a meat-eating mammal of the Eocene era. Fifty million years ago, the mesonychid flourished in Europe, living in humid zones along the ancient ocean that covered the area of the current Mediterranean Sea. This terrain was very favorable to its survival after the large reptiles of the Cretaceous period had become extinct, and it also lived in Asia and North America.

Little by little, the mesonychid began to spend more time in the water than on land, and so it adapted to its new surroundings. Imagine that you are watching a film of the hunting scene I've just described, which was miraculously made in that distant bygone era. Believe it or not, this big fish-eating wolf you see diving, catching fish, and devouring its prey is the ancestor of the whales and dolphins that populate our oceans today.

I stop a minute to check the effect my story is having on my audience: a dozen chubby-cheeked children, their faces aglow in the light of hurricane lamps, sitting in the mess room of the *Fleur de Lampaul* en route for the Azores. There is a long silence. My little sailor-reporters stare at me with big round eyes. They have just ridden out a nasty windstorm in the Bay of Biscay, which hit us just a few hours after we'd shipped out from the Isle de Yeu. They are shaken and exhausted. They have taken off their slickers and hung them to drip in the closets, but their hair is still full of sea spume. There is salt in their eyebrows and their hands are full of blisters from pulling on the rough old ropes of our historic vessel, now converted to an "oceanographic sailboat for children." Our sailors acquitted themselves well, and the four adults on board are proud of them. We'll have a seasoned crew to look for sperm whales by the time we get to the Azores.

After the bad weather had passed and the calm had returned, the captain and second captain remained on deck and the rest of us went down to dinner. A hearty meal of veal and rice with gravy reinvigorated battered bodies that had suffered through six long hours of storm. The bravest among us took dessert, and a spurt of questions quickly followed: How much do sperm whales weigh? How big are they? How many will there be at Horta? *How much, how big, how many?* Children's questions are loaded with "how manys," and I've never been good at memorizing numbers. One of them asked me if I knew how long whales had been living on the planet. I couldn't resist the temptation to tell them the story of the very strange wolf that, once upon a time, lived in the Eocene era.

Once they'd gotten over their stupefaction, the budding sailors of the *Fleur de Lampaul* took out their handsome ship logs and began to take notes. Embarking for several months on this splendid sailing ship, classified as a historical monument, they all had willingly agreed to accept a moral contract: upon their return, they would share everything they had discovered while they were on board with those who had remained behind. Since they had agreed to show and tell, they didn't want to forget anything, especially not a good story. And the story of cetacean evolution is among the strangest of all, despite its complications and mysterious, shady areas. The interest of research lies in the unknowns. Cetacean evolution is an extraordinary adventure, a phenomenal metamorphosis worthy of the best special effects in any science fiction film, a mutation that takes place in the wink of an eye, at least on the scale of geological time—a mere few tens of millions of years.

In appearance, the hoofed wolf of the Eocene era has nothing in common with the blue whale, the largest animal the planet has ever known, which reaches a weight of 150 tons and can measure up to thirty meters long. Nevertheless, the sciences of paleontology, genetics, and biochemistry have discovered the characteristics of this meat-eating ancestor in the anatomy of whales today. Furthermore, fossils dating back to half a million years ago permit us to trace ancestral links between modern cetaceans and other hoofed animals going back to time immemorial, including animals more ancient than the mesonychid itself.

The best-known ancestors of modern-day cetaceans are the Archaeoceti, which probably descended from the mesonychid. They evolved in a decisive fashion over a period of about 10 million years. Scientists suppose they lived similarly to the way sea otters and sea lions live today. Their tails must have flattened and changed their shape to beaters, but the debate is still open on how and when their posterior paws regressed. Certain fossils of the smaller Archaeoceti show vestiges of these members. Morphological and physiological changes then rapidly followed as the animal adapted to the imperatives of an essentially aquatic life, even though these primitive whales certainly continued to live partially on land, where they had to return in order to reproduce.

As the hearing of this animal adapted, its eardrum became modified so it could hear underwater. The rest of its head closely resembled that of other land mammals. This is especially true of its teeth, which consisted of incisors, canines, and molars. Its jaw grew longer, the better to securely grasp its prey. A well-defined rostrum developed, its nostrils drew back to the top of the head, and its sinuses enlarged. The eyes and kidneys adapted themselves to the salinity of seawater, and a layer of fat grew beneath the skin to help it endure the cold. Slowly, its fur disappeared in favor of a smooth, slick skin ideal for penetrating water.

One of these creatures, the zeuglodont, is very well

known. It measured between fifteen and twenty meters long, and weighed over fifteen tons. For a long time, fossils of this animal, which was shaped like a serpent, caused us to believe it was a reptile, but the discovery of a skull, which was so small that it represented only 7 percent of the total length of its body, permitted scientists to definitively reclassify it as a mammal. Its back limbs were small, reduced to short flippers. Although its spinal column does not appear to have been strong enough to support the tail movements of modern-day cetaceans, the zeuglodont's agility permitted it to wriggle with great suppleness through the shallow waters of its feeding grounds. Its teeth were devised to seize its prey and crush its bones. Its blowhole, close to the upper extremity of the muzzle, allowed it to breathe while barely grazing the surface: all it had to do was stick the end of its nose above the water.

About 30 million years ago, Archaeoceti doubtlessly ruled the sea, but an emerging generation had already begun to challenge their superiority. The truth is, we still don't know whether they disappeared as a result of environmental changes or became extinct on their own. In any case, their successors were the beginning of our modern-day Odontoceti, or tooth whales, and Mysticeti, or baleen whales, which have plates of baleen, or whalebone.

The members of these two suborders obviously adapted better to aquatic life than their ancient cousin. First, tooth whales are better hunters, thanks to their system of echolocation, which allows them to orient themselves and locate their prey in near darkness, and baleen whales are capable of filtering seawater, which allows them to ingurgitate enormous quantities of food. But the factor that really determined their advantage is their ability to give birth at sea, and thus no longer to have to return to land.

How did they go about such transformations? How did they succeed? Nothing is certain, but they must have been able to take advantage of the distribution of marine currents and the modifications in ecological conditions brought about by global variations in ocean levels. Cetacean evolution may well be linked to disturbances in the Southern Hemisphere during this period, and in particular to the progressive dislocation of Gondwanaland, the Southern supercontinent that fractured apart when Australia, South America, and Africa, formerly connected to Antarctica, drifted to the north. The breakup of Gondwanaland, from which the current position of the continents derives, permitted cetaceans to conquer new seas and benefit from the food reserves they found there.

At this point their teeth underwent modification, forming either the sharp, canine denture typical of the majority of toothed whales today, or giving rise to the plates of whalebone characteristic of baleen whales. They developed a waterproof means of sealing off their nostrils, lost all neck mobility, and progressively acquired the torpedo-shaped profile hydrodynamics so favors. Their bodies reabsorbed their back legs and pelvis, so that nothing remained but a tiny pair of pelvic bones. Their tail flukes became the formidable means of propulsion we know from whales today. In a number of species, the appearance of a fibrous dorsal fin helped to maintain lateral equilibrium. The skulls of tooth whales underwent further metamorphosis in accordance with the needs of echolocation. Those of the baleen whales evolved differently. Their foreheads grew considerably larger toward the front, causing their jawbones to elongate and resulting in immense jaws that facilitate the gathering of plankton.

Finally, about 25 million years ago, squalodonts, dolphins with sharklike teeth, appeared. These animals probably resembled the pilot whales of today, with blowholes located close to the top of their craniums. Once common throughout the entire Southern Hemisphere, these creatures finally disappeared, in turn, 10 or 15 million years ago with the rise of modern dolphins. Squalodonts were supplanted by neighboring families, in particular by Ziphiidae, or beaked whales, which are great lovers of squid. Such a diet so little requires well-developed teeth that beaked whales today only have a single pair, planted in their lower jaw. These teeth most certainly play no role in grasping their prey, for they are lacking in the females, which nevertheless have no difficulty in obtaining food. The same kind of adaptation is seen in sperm whales, which have lost the teeth on their upper jaw. It was during this same period that rorquals—minke whales, Bryde's whales, sei whales, fin whales, and blue whales—acquired their elongated "muzzle" and developed horny strips between their teeth, which then atrophied.

Today cetaceans are still subdivided into two principal suborders: Mysticeti, or baleen whales, and Odontoceti, or tooth whales. The dozen families they comprise are made up of at least eighty different species. The baleen whales include the larger right whale, the pygmy right whale, the bowhead whale, the gray whale, and all the more streamlined rorquals, a genus of baleen whales with throat grooves and a small pointed fin. Classified as tooth whales are the sperm whales, the narwhal and the white whale or beluga, all the beaked and bottlenose whales, ocean dolphins, river dolphins, and porpoises.

Stop! One after the other, the budding sailors on the *Fleur de Lampaul* were losing track of the story. Among the youngest, those who still were able to fight back sleep were yawning so hard their eyes were full of tears. The bigger ones had cramps in their fingers and could no longer hold their pencils. So I halted my lecture, sparing them the details of scientific controversy. They had surely understood the essential point: in permitting the evolution of marine mammals, nature had fashioned sublime creatures whose every leap above the surface, whose every dive and turn in the limpid waters where they fish or play, is full of power and grace. There would be plenty of time later to discuss the sperm whale's incredible ability to suspend its breath, the "song" of the whales, the reasons that whales became so gigantic, the whistles or "clicks" that dolphins make, and the strange way they perceive their world and possibly the humans who are bold enough to approach them in their natural element. In a few days, we would be diving with sperm whales and Atlantic spotted dolphins in the Azores. I had not yet finished answering all those "hows" and "whys."

I don't know if the young sailors I accompanied on the *Fleur de Lampaul* and those I've continued to meet at La Rochelle remember everything I've told them, but one thing I am sure of: not a single one of them has ever forgotten the Eocene "wolf" with a fish between its teeth, pummeling the mud of a swamp with its hooves.

Although many uncertainties still remain concerning the lineage of our modern-day cetaceans, although genetics are revolutionizing some of our ideas in paleontology and the current classification of marine mammals is often subjected to challenge, one thing is certain: dolphins and whales had a furry, four-legged ancestor who gamboled along the seashore. Theirs was an extraordinary evolution, and the transformations they underwent to adapt to a marine environment still exceed our wildest imagination.

Seeing beyond Appearances

G reat! I'm going to collect seawater samples for the
lab!"

The headlands of Brittany offer more perilous challenges, but my friend was enthusiastic by nature. A fellow
student at Brest in the 1970s, she was always ready for anything. The instructors could ask her to do any kind of work,
even the most disagreeable, and she always carried out her
task as energetically as if the fate of science depended on it.
Earlier, a researcher in biology had invited my friend and me
to visit his lab. He was a nice guy, but the place itself was sor-
did—one small room with a single narrow window, clouded
with the accumulation of a decade of dirt. Hundreds of
vials were lined up along the shelves. There was not enough
room to budge. Tucking our hands behind our backs, we
stood as straight as ramrods, barely daring to turn around.
After touching on the significance of his work, our researcher
brandished a test tube that contained, to all appearances,
some ordinary sand, and cried out: "What you see here is
my whole life's work! Every year I discover amongst these
grains of sand a minute crustacean that no one has ever described before!"

I thought I was going to throw up. But a smile of ecstasy was plastered across my friend's face. She thought it was marvelous; I felt the need to escape. True, I wanted to work in the field of marine biology—but not at any price. Although I understood the usefulness of long, fastidious research, I didn't envision myself counting the hairs on the legs of sea lice for the rest of my life in the hope of finding one with two or three more hairs than the rest. My friend never asked herself the question: everything was just "great." When a professor asked her to go to Le Conquet to collect five liters of seawater for his experiments, she blushed with pleasure and murmured "great" again. She asked me to go with her, as I was one of the rare students with a car in those days. I was driving an old two-horsepower jalopy, which had the added attraction of being a convertible. This made it easy to bring along my windsurfing board—one of the first in France—and navigate the waves for a few hours after each of our "field days," as we called the sessions of practical training we got on the beach.

So I drove my friend to her appointment with the seawater in the channel at Le Four. I remember she was wearing boots and had put a slicker on over her sailor's jersey. She had overdone it a bit for October, even if the sky did look menacing. But she was so full of joy that I didn't have the heart to make the slightest remark. Nevertheless, once we arrived in Le Conquet, I found a pretext to leave her to accomplish her mission alone, agreeing to come and pick her up on the jetty two hours later. I made use of the time to drive around the cove toward the cliffs in the north, where I scanned the beach at Les Blancs-Sablons with my binoculars.

A few weeks earlier, I'd found the cadaver of a washed-up common dolphin, from which I'd been able to take a few teeth samples. This time, the beach was empty. I retraced my path and went to pick up my friend. I found her seated on an abandoned crate, her container in her hand, looking vexed. I asked her what was the matter.

"I went over to a fisherman to ask him if he would show me the best place to take my sample. I was hoping he would take me out to the edge of the bay in his boat. He pointed to the far end of the quay and said, 'There's a spigot there. It's seawater. You can take some, but don't drink any, because it will make you sick.'"

I still don't know how I kept from laughing. I actually think she was sincerely unhappy, and I would have hurt her if I had made fun of her. After this disappointment, she ended up admitting that everything about scientific research wasn't so "great" after all. The results can have tremendous repercussions and are sometimes big enough to revolutionize our conception of the planet, or even the universe. But the road to achieving them can be deadly boredom for anyone whose soul is not in it. My friend's enthusiasm merely wavered—a lesson learned at little expense. But sometimes disappointments are more serious, and failures can be bitter. One bad choice and the damage is irreparable. It is better to follow the pull of your own heart, your inner voice, and your personal convictions than to follow in someone else's footsteps. All of which does not exclude bouts of enthusiasm—to the contrary.

My interest in cetology was born in the days when my friend was collecting those lab samples. Before that time, I knew nothing about it. Like the majority of the population, I remembered Flipper's tricks, but the exotic heroics of a televised dolphin had not impressed me. Dolphins were not yet being used as symbols by organizations dedicated to the protection of wildlife, or by the retailer down the street. They got little press, and scientists were still in the dark, although they had conducted research and discovered some of the extraordinary things of which these animals are capable. One of these struck me with stupefaction when I learned about it, and it continues to amaze me today.

Sperm whales, orcas, and dolphins orient themselves in their natural surroundings in a way that is almost unique in the world of living things. It's a gift of nature, a miracle of evolution so perfect that we still haven't managed to completely understand and analyze it. It is a revelation that has transformed our entire approach to marine mammals.

Cetaceans have rid themselves of every outward sign of the exterior ear—or almost every sign. The ear flap has completely disappeared: once again, this appendage was not designed for hydrodynamics. Their ears are nothing but little holes, often situated just behind their eyes, and their ear canals are no larger than two or three millimeters in diameter. Thus not much remains, but the little that does must nevertheless have its uses. An ear filled with air is not very efficient in the water, however; and, conversely, an ear filled with water is not very useful above the surface. A stopper of horny wax obstructs the inner ear of certain baleen whales, fostering the transmission of sound underwater (and perhaps rendering them deaf out of water); dolphins, by contrast, are not thus equipped. We are still trying to

discover what they can hear both above and below the surface—all the more so since sound waves are disrupted as
they pass from air to water. The hypothesis has been put
forth that their ear canals are permanently open and filled
with water. In this case, they would hear correctly only
underwater. Nevertheless, it seems as if certain species are
able to perceive sounds after surfacing, so their ears must let
in a little air. According to another hypothesis, their ear
canals actually serve no function at all. They are nothing but
superfluous reminders of their former life on dry land. This
would explain why the ear canals of certain species are completely obstructed.

In an effort to understand how all this works, researchers
decided to deprive a bottlenose dolphin of its sight in order
to make it rely on its other senses. Small patches of rubber,
held in place by suction, were placed over its eyes in order to
blind it temporarily. The dolphin was accustomed to receiv-
ing a reward for locating a particular, well-defined object in
its pool after swimming through an obstacle course. At the
signal, the dolphin started off "with its eyes shut," avoiding
the obstacles with disconcerting ease. And then it went
straight for the trophy! Either it was magic, or the dolphin
had a secret that scientists had finally managed to uncover.

Throughout its course, the dolphin kept emitting short
series of sounds, turning its head back and forth a few degrees from left to right, and with increasing rapidity as it
encountered unexpected obstacles in its path. It became obvious that delphinids had developed a particular means of
using sound waves, and that our subject was orienting itself
through echolocation—a system that is unique, extremely

sophisticated, and fabulously precise. Bats possess a similar gift, but it seems that cetaceans are alone in using it underwater. The challenge was to understand how it functioned in their natural environment. Biology and acoustics both came to the rescue, but the answers they offered still need to be refined today after thirty years of experimentation.

Sound waves travel better than light waves in water. It is understandable that a system based on sound would become more evolved than the sense of sight, since this would be more useful and effective in assuring the survival of the species. When a dolphin thrusts forward, it emits low-frequency sounds that travel long distances. At other times, it produces ultrasounds or high frequencies, which diffuse over short distances. In this way, the animal sweeps the area before it, so nothing escapes its notice. Any obstacle the sound waves encounter reflects them back to the dolphin, which captures and analyzes them. It knows how far away the object is, and its shape, nature, texture, and density. This is why the dolphin's system of echolocation has been compared to a ship's sonar, an acoustical device developed to locate objects underwater, which permits us to "see" where the light rays essential to vision do not penetrate. This apparatus, like the sonar dolphins use, "sees" by analyzing the reflection of sound waves rather than light waves. The echolocation system of Odontoceti is highly perfected; we now know that it allows them to distinguish a piece of copper from a piece of aluminum with an identical shape, and to recognize two objects, both made of lead, that barely differ from each other.

Lacking vocal chords, dolphins emit sounds by using air

sacs, which they play like a wind instrument. These sacs are located beneath the blowholes and open into the nasal passage. The animal uses the air it inhales to produce whistling or clicking sounds by passing the air from one sac to the other. Sound waves reflect off the concave frontal wall of its skull before concentrating in the convex part of its head, or melon. Filled with oil, the melon acts like a convergent lens that orients the beams of sound waves in the direction the animal desires. In the sperm whale, the melon has reached gigantic proportions. This spermaceti organ, as it is called, weighs several tons and takes up almost the entirety of its enormous head. It is probable that tooth whales also use their larynx to send other types of vibrations that we also sometimes manage to hear.

While this system of emission is surprising, the system of reception is nothing short of a marvel. Tooth whales not only perceive sound waves with their ears: in the water, they receive them through their entire bodies. To sort out the hundreds of echoes with which they are bombarded, dolphins have developed a high-performance analytical tool known as tympanic bullae, where the inner and middle parts of the ear are located. These are very compact, bony formations suspended in the skull cavity and protected by a pocket filled with a spongy mixture of mucus and oil.

The ear canal, extremely narrow and often obstructed, is not the only means of capturing echoes, for a dolphin whose ears have been blocked can find its way without difficulty. In fact, sound waves spread the most easily through its lower jaw. Its mandible is formed by a hollow bone whose cavity is filled with a kind of very fine oil, similar to that

found in the melon. Vibrations conducted through this oil
are transmitted to the internal ear, situated just next to the
articulation of the jaw. These vibrations reach the brain
thanks to a highly developed auditory nerve capable of
transmitting nearly limitless amounts of the most complex
and diverse information.

When a dolphin becomes particularly interested in an
object, it approaches while emitting clicks of increasing rapidity and higher frequency, lightly turning its head from
left to right so the beam of sound waves will sweep across
the object from every direction. It then touches the object
with the extreme point of its jaw in order to directly pick up
the returning echo. It is probable that the dolphin thus ac-
quires extraordinarily precise information concerning not
only the shape and outer texture of the object, but also its
density and internal structure. Like an ultrasound that reveals the image of a fetus in its mother's womb, so the dolphin, thanks to its sonar, can no doubt tell what I ate at my
last meal.

Thus tooth whales have perfected a system of echolocation based, as its name indicates, on sound waves, which
allows them to pick out the features of the ocean floor several thousand meters beneath the surface and to identify
their prey in the ocean darkness. They see with their ears.
Over the course of thousands of years, as their sonar gradually developed, their anatomy and their physiology were
transformed. Anatomically, the skull bones made room for
masses of oil in the melon and mandible, the vocal cords
atrophied, air sacs appeared, and the larynx transformed itself; physiologically, their sense of hearing acquired another

function, and the areas of their skulls associated with hearing changed their dimensions. Since baleen whales did not undergo these transformations, it is believed they are not equipped with a system of echolocation. They nevertheless do vocalize often and use low-frequency sounds that travel for dozens of kilometers. It is probable that the sounds they emit in the course of their migration give them information not only about the whereabouts of other whales but also about the map of the ocean floor, and that certain outstanding features of the map act as orientation points from which they take their direction.

I still remember my amazement the first time someone described to me this barely imaginable adaptation to environment. The discovery unveiled a universe of which I was totally ignorant, for twenty years ago popular works on whales were rare, and for my own part, I was convinced that dolphins were exotic, tropical creatures. As for the orcas, or killer whales, so familiar to children today, I barely knew they existed. Like all my friends, I would have sworn that seals never left their ice floes, and that there was not the slightest chance of glimpsing a whale's back anywhere off the coast of Europe. And then I discovered that dolphins were crossing just off the coast of Brittany, that baleen whales were also sighted there, and that seals were perched on our rocks—and all this was just half an hour's drive from the university. I felt myself more and more attracted to the cliffs and beaches, far from the labs with their rows of sad little test tubes filled with "a whole life's work."

My initiation to ornithology, my first passion, had already given me a taste for observing animals in their natural habitat. But birds did not attract me the way mammals do. Perhaps this is because all mammals, myself included, are conscious of belonging to the same group, so that makes me feel closer to them. I discovered the cetaceans, with their extravagant physiology and their mysterious behavior, just at the right time. This was the truer in that cetology was an area in which everything was yet to be done, and this suited my temperament to a T. I've always preferred thorny paths to comfortable boulevards. The vocation of research implies an instinctive curiosity, an irrepressible desire to go where no one has been before, an almost uncontrollable attraction for what we do not know or understand. It requires the exuberance of a child's imagination—love of play, inventing, making paths that never existed before—because the trodden path does not lead to discovery. Researchers shed light where the rest of humankind can barely see.

Bit by bit, I incited my fellow bird-watchers to direct their binoculars toward the ocean and the exotic creatures cavorting in its waters. They were quickly seduced—after all, the gaze of a seal is much more touching than that of a seagull. Soon, while we were still students, we created a study group to examine animals washed ashore, one of the very first ever to operate in France. Obviously, we hoped to study not only dead animals, but also those that were alive and well and leaping near the bows of our boats when we went sailing in our leisure hours. It was a wager on the future, made with the carefree attitude of youth. It was also a bet on the animals we were readying ourselves to study, for if we already loved them before we knew them, we also were probably asking ourselves if the dolphins, with their special

way of sensing things, would find anything to love in us.
There are so many legends about dolphins helping human
beings, rescues that seem to indicate that they are not indifferent toward us, that I had to get a closer look and see for
myself what it was all about.

After all, since they live in an aquatic environment while
we live surrounded by air, they don't often see us, they can
probably barely hear us, and they rarely smell us. What do
they think of us when we join them in their element? They
are sensitive to the slightest chemical substance dissolved
in the water: this is how the males pick up the sexual
pheromones the females disseminate in the waves to signal
they are ready to mate. What do we taste like? When dolphins discover an intriguing object, they observe it, try to
figure out all its details through echolocation, touch it with
the tip of their chin, or take it in their mouth. Dolphins discover their likes and dislikes in their own way. What picture
do they draw of us with that supersonar of theirs that nothing escapes? They don't stop at the surface of things but
"see" beyond appearances. Maybe their sonar penetrates to
the bone, to the heart. From there, it's not so far to think they
may be able to know our emotions.

Finally, and this is my good luck, it seems they are at
least as curious as I am. I observe them only because they
permit themselves be observed. Every time I do, there
comes a moment when I ask myself who is observing
whom. Our encounter cannot take place except through
mutual consent. I go toward them as much as they come toward me: I can get back in my boat where they cannot join
me, just as they can escape to the depths of the ocean where

I cannot follow them. They are just as free as I am to accept or reject the relationship our encounter establishes. As long as it continues, I have to believe there is something in it for both of us.

Swimming with Children and Three Hundred Dolphins
The Voyage of the Fleur de Lampaul

When I'm at sea, I like to keep the night watch. And on the *Fleur de Lampaul*, I like to keep the night watch with the children. I am amused by the sleepy expressions on their faces as they put on their slickers and equipment before going up to the deck, by the way they pull their hats down all the way over their eyebrows. Night impresses them; little inclined to talk, they cock their ears in the attempt to hear the wind welling up in the darkness. Often the whales are there—we are, after all, in their "territory"—but most of the time there is only the murmur of water against the hull and the whisper of wind in the sails.

Still heavy with sleep, the children sit on the damp wood, knees tucked under their chins, hands wrapped around their ankles. They shiver and swallow hot chocolate in short little sips, their gazes lost in the stars, while the *Fleur,* her sails shortened, travels around in a circle. By remaining in the same area, tomorrow we'll find sperm whales and dolphins again. All around us the moonlight illuminates a misty, shifting universe. The sea at night is not for humans, unless it is viewed from the deck of a ship where nocturnal terrors can be defied in relative security. But this unique time weaves strong and invisible ties, creating a sense of complicity that will prove to be a precious asset when the moment comes to dive among the animals at dawn.

Some of the children sleep on the sly, others come over to me asking in whispers if they are really going to see dolphins, if they are really going to get in the water with them, if it will be hard, if it will last a long time, if it won't be scary to swim with them. We have hours before us with nothing to do but talk, with long periods of silence to give the words time enough to grow and nourish their dreams. In the darkness their voices move me. As I listen to them, I imagine their desires and fears. They remind me that I, too, once was twelve years old, and that I dreamed, like them, but beneath other stars. It was a time when Cousteau's camera had just transformed the horrific abyss into a wonderland, when no one yet imagined that common mortals could pass through to the other side of the mirror. Back then, thirty years ago, factory ships in the Southern seas were killing whales by the thousands, and porpoises snitching sardines from fishing nets were hunted down with rifles off the coast of France. Unlike cats and dogs, horses, and a few birds, cetaceans had not yet been admitted to the pantheon of animals thought to be "man's friend." We were not yet capturing orcas and bottlenose dolphins for aquatic circuses, not yet driving them to neurosis for the sake of making a splash with crowds of curious onlookers.

When the future adventure seekers on the *Fleur de Lampaul* first came to meet me at the Center for Research on Marine Mammals, I already felt attracted to the project Charles Hervé-Gruyer, the owner of the *Fleur*, had conceived. He was ready to embark a dozen young sailor-reporters between the ages of twelve and fifteen on a voyage to discover the planet. This project included exploring the world of cetaceans, a subject that was very apt to interest me. But I do not, a priori, feel the calling to incite my peers, much less children, to approach marine mammals physically. Too many experiments with the goal of establishing a so-called contact between humans and dolphins have had disastrous effects, especially for the animals. The same sometimes holds true for the mental health of those who participate in the experiments.

Nevertheless, in our very first discussions at the Center, the team that Charles Hervé-Gruyer had put together began to calm my fears. I talked with the young people, I described the skeletons of dolphins we had carefully reconstituted from washed-up specimens, I made them take a tour of the organ samples we keep in our laboratory, I spoke to them at length about what it is like to work under the microscope, cooped up in a narrow room, or to stand on the deck of a ship staring at an empty sea through a pair of binoculars. I foregrounded all the worst aspects of a scientist's work, and yet their response was unexpectedly sympathetic. They were supposed to come for an hour or two, but every time they visited the Center, they stayed the whole day long. They questioned me, took notes and photographs, and learned as much as they could, accumulating knowledge with a view to future encounters with dolphins and whales. I saw that their organizers were just as serious as they were. They had undertaken a project in the spirit of true pedagogy, imagining an intelligent approach to cetaceans in their natural habitat. I invested a bit of my own time and was amply repaid by the curiosity shining in the children's eyes, and their ever-pertinent questions.

Later, when they asked me to accompany them on their expeditions, I hesitated because of lack of time, even though I had always considered it my duty to leave the lab as often as possible to explain the results of our research to newcomers. To my way of thinking, such availability is far too rare among scientists. In the end, the children's motivation, passion, and thirst for knowledge convinced me to help them pull some strings to arrange a meeting with the whales.

Later still, like every other passionate sailor who ever set foot aboard that wonderful ship, I fell in love with the *Fleur de Lampaul*. It is a national treasure.

The expedition to the Azores in 1991 took place during summer vacation. There was no need for the children to pursue their studies on board, which left us more time to learn about marine animals in the best of conditions. In addition to its beauty, the *Fleur* is an excellent floating observatory. A nineteenth-century sailing ship once used to transport sand, it is robust, spacious, quiet, stable, and high on the water. The friendly yet responsible atmosphere on board incited us all to do whatever we could to provide our youthful adventurers with what they had come looking for—as long as the animals also wanted to cooperate.

The back of the mid-Atlantic mountain chain surges up from the depths of the ocean, breaking the surface fifteen hundred kilometers from Lisbon. The nine Portuguese islands that constitute the Azores are among its highest summits. Cold currents originating from the bottom cross warm ones from a branch of the Gulf Stream in the vicinity of these volcanic islands. The water is temperate and the

weather is capricious even in summer, but this is one area
on the planet where cetaceans are sure to be seen, swimming
in waters that the surrounding islands shelter from the heaviest swells. The sperm whales are there, of course: it is they
who created the glory of the islands—Pico, Faïal, and Saõ
Miguel, where generations of harpooners known for their incredible recklessness followed one after the other, up until the
time that whaling was prohibited. Bottlenose dolphins are
also present in great number, along with common dolphins,
Risso's dolphins, short-finned pilot whales, and, above all,
Atlantic spotted dolphins. More rarely, it is possible to see
rorquals: killer whales (orcas), false killer whales, and
Sowerby's beaked whales.

The spectacle of mountains plunging straight into the
sea and rising up into the mist is a source of constant pleasure in the Azores, but it is simply out of the question to
anchor near their shores, for the water is far too deep. If we
were to be ready to go to work at dawn, the *Fleur* couldn't
leave the area where the animals would appear. According
to the winds and currents, we let her gently drift or tacked
throughout the night. Although I am unable to offer any
rigorous explanations, our best contacts with cetaceans take
place immediately after sunrise. At dawn, when the sea is
still, the animals are apparently sensitive to the peacefulness
and seem calmer themselves. They accept our boats, whose
motors they hear from afar, with no sign of surprise, nor are
they surprised by our presence. We do not understand why
they are most convivial in the hours just after dawn, because
we don't yet know the rhythms by which different species
live. Certain animals that only feed at night may experience
a period of rest in the morning, when they are freer for

encounters or games. But others, known to hunt both day and night, are just as peaceful, and just as curious about us. For whatever reason, dolphins most often come calling at daybreak.

But they are also quite capable of acting aloof. Dolphins refuse to fit the categories that a literature created for "dolphin lovers" often tries to impose on them. Pompous systems and mystical claims are reductive in any case. Dolphins are highly evolved mammals whose intelligence has permitted them to go beyond the droning uniformity of bees or ants, as amazing as these creatures may be in their own right. From one hive to another, from one anthill to another, insects of the same species all act pretty much the same. But not dolphins. They are like those grammars whose every rule is accompanied by a long list of exceptions. All attempts to classify them according to ironclad laws of behavior have failed. Every study shows that whatever we learn from one group of dolphins does not apply to the next. And all the wild imaginings about dolphins being almost human—or more than human, close to divine—are equally without a future. While dolphins are considered social animals that live in families and groups, some remain solitary for long periods of time, sometimes for several years, living in the same territory. Many scientists consider them as fortuitous cases, and thus negligible. Others, gullible fools or sorry profiteers of cheap mythology, sometimes call them "ambassadors," as if they carried a message from their "people" to ours, or played an intermediary role between the human and the divine.

Fortunately, dolphins themselves will never know the heavy freight of commerce they carry on their backs, or the fantasies with which we've adorned them. Such excesses and blatherings only go to show that our knowledge is still very limited, that in certain domains we haven't even begun, and that ignorance has always been the most fertile ground for illusion. When science cannot explain, the field is wide open to imagination.

The more our research advances, the more we discover that the behavior of species, stocks, pods, and even individuals differs from one to the other. We are still very far from being able to formulate rules, if rules indeed are what we want. For the moment, we are happy to discover more and more new possibilities, abilities, strategies, and techniques that a dolphin uses to live in its own way, like an artist who creates an infinite variety of hues from a painter's palette. The behavior of orcas, for example, among the most popular cetaceans all over the world, still remains a mystery to us. Some pods master skills of which others remain completely ignorant. Certain of them feed on fish, while others eat seals. Within any one group, some individuals are more gifted than others in approaching their prey, camouflaging themselves or even voluntarily beaching themselves to capture a young elephant seal or penguin. Bottlenose dolphins found in Florida live differently than do those along the English coast, while those along the shores of Brittany behave otherwise than the ones found near Arcachon in southern France. Starting in 1996, we began to study dolphins in the Charente straits because chances are that their behavior demonstrates yet a different strategy. And in fact, preliminary results do not conform to those obtained with dolphins near the neighboring Isle de Sein or in the Arcachon basin.

Every time we observe them anew, we get a new surprise:

in one place, the animals show up every day; in another, they appear only in good weather—or only when the weather is bad. Where do they go when we can no longer observe them? Whenever the surface is even slightly troubled, their presence becomes difficult to detect. Sometimes they seem to like enormous swells in the depths off a rocky coast; at other times, they daily navigate delicate passes, hunting between sandbanks where the bottom emerges at low tide. In the straits of Charente, the water is a maximum of thirty meters deep, and the sea is often calm. Nothing is fixed, nothing is definitively known. Henceforth, any report about dolphins, be it more or less scientific, will not only document the particular species of dolphin under observation, but also note the place and date in order to draw conclusions relative to this specific time and place, and avoid deceptive generalizations. Experience has taught us to suspect the certitudes of the past.

If dolphins are "ambassadors" for anything, they are certainly role models for modesty. This is an innate quality in many children, and it is strictly cultivated on the *Fleur.* Like adults, children want to have the answer to everything, but they still know how to ask questions and are open-minded enough to come up with new dreams when the old ones no longer fit reality.

When we began diving with the dolphins, I asked the children to forget all received ideas about the animals they were about to approach, and to act as if they were the first humans ever to pay them a visit. The interns on the *Fleur* are no different from any other lover of marine mammals— they want to understand everything, but first they are there to observe, ask questions, and bear witness, while accepting that they don't have the answer for everything. They assume nothing and hope for everything. This is perhaps the correct definition of the "scientific method."

In the Azores, our observation always begins on deck: we have to locate the cetaceans after having passed the night circling in the zone where they are found. At dawn, a member of the team charged with locating the animals climbs the mast to the crow's nest, while the divers designated to accompany me get ready: flippers, masks, and snorkels all are near at hand. As soon as the sun's first rays sparkle across the surface of the ocean, we usually sight the animals, and the captain heads out toward them.

One morning, we glimpsed furtive shadows flitting to the starboard side. I picked up the binoculars and directed them toward a group of slender, torpedo-like shapes that seemed to be pursuing a school of flying fish. They were Atlantic spotted dolphins, about two meters long, which are easily confused with young bottlenose dolphins. Outside the water, it is difficult to distinguish the little spots that speckle their bellies, and later, as they grow older, their steel-gray backs as well. They also have narrower beaks than bottlenose dolphins. Lively and playful, they are also voracious hunters, very partial to catching squid in the depths or chasing surface fish while swimming in the company of albacore tuna. Furthermore, they are well armed: their jaws are adorned with as many as 160 little conical teeth.

I asked the children to get ready while our skipper reduced our speed. Would the dolphins continue on their way, or would our presence incite their curiosity? For a few seconds we saw nothing more, then suddenly a dozen dolphins passed by us, this time to port side. I was unable to say whether it was the same group, but they showed no sign of being upset, and even less of aggressiveness. The *Fleur* seemed to fascinate them; they kept changing speeds, allowing us to catch up, then taking off again. It was classic dolphin behavior, but for some reason I had the feeling that we were in for a surprise.

"In we go!"

The names of two girls had come up when we drew lots: Morvana, from the Gulf of Morbihan, and Siobhan, from Cornwall. Both of them were twelve years old. I asked them to be very attentive, because I had the feeling that the animals could be more numerous than we thought. We'd seen ten of them, but there were probably two or three times as many. Each time we dive, I take only two children. This is first of all for safety's sake, so I can keep an eye on them and be able to help in case a problem comes up. Diving without a tank in the middle of the Atlantic, even when it's undertaken with the necessary precautions, all the same has nothing in common with taking a swim near the beach. But we also limit our numbers out of respect for our hosts, in order not to disturb them.

After climbing down the ladder over the hull, we gently and silently slipped into the water. "Going to see the dolphins" by jumping overboard with a big splash was out of the question.

"Of course," said Morvana, "I would never enter the house of someone I didn't know, kicking in the door without warning!" Her spontaneous remark proved to me that the children had understood how to go about their upcoming encounter.

The dolphins were still there. Usually the young ones, who are the least wary, behave like curious, alert, carefree adolescents. They can be crafty as well, because sometimes their conspicuous presence near a boat is designed to detract attention from the rest of the family. The females and their young thus remain apart. Such was not the case this time, for the pod came back to us when we'd barely done a few strokes. The two girls instinctively grabbed my hands, one on the left, the other on the right, and we floated, immobile. The dolphins filed under us, at a depth of less than three meters, then a male turned on his side to observe us. The three of us still were floating, all holding hands. We were wearing colorful swimsuits, flippers, masks, and snorkels. What a strange-looking six-legged creature we must have seemed to the dolphins looking at this spectacle!

In the beginning, the eye of the dolphin was like that of any other land mammal, probably comparable to our own. Because their eyes were adapted to see on land, when dolphins became aquatic, their vision would have been blurry. In the water, the image of an object no longer is formed on the retina, but behind it. Human beings correct this problem by wearing masks that keep our eyes in contact with the air, but cetaceans over the course of their evolution developed eye muscles that are strong enough to change the form of their lens. This became almost spherical, like that of fish, and the eyeball flattened out as their sight adjusted to a marine environment. By thus bettering their capacity to adapt, dolphins can see just as well underwater as above the surface.

Seawater is particularly corrosive, and a dolphin's eyes
are protected by a thick, gelatinous mucus continually se-
creted through special glands. It covers the entire cornea, creating the impression that the animals are crying when they
are out of the water. In fact, they would be hard-pressed to
shed a single tear, for dolphins do not have lachrymal glands.
They do have eyelids, which are without lashes, and which
they close for the most part when they sleep.

Dolphins, like all other members of the tooth whale
family, essentially have a one-eyed vision of the world. Ordinarily, since their eyes are situated on the sides of their
heads, they see with only one eye at a time. But the smaller
delphinids' lower field of vision is binocular for about twenty
degrees, which permits them to have stereoscopic, or three-
dimensional, vision. Thus, when they wish to distinguish us
clearly when we are out of the water, they position themselves vertically with their heads above the surface and look
at us by directing their gaze beneath their jaws.

Light waves travel poorly beneath the water, and darkness rapidly increases with the distance from the surface.
We have learned that dolphins possess a reflective shield,
situated behind the retina, that facilitates night vision by
reflecting light like a mirror. Species like beaked whales,
sperm whales, and certain pilot whales, which dive to the
depths of the ocean hunting squid, have weaker vision than
the small delphinids but seem able to detect the lumines-
cent organs of their prey at a depth of two hundred meters
or more. Humpback whales have extremely mobile eyes
whose pupils dilate greatly in the darkness to capture the
least ray of light but contract into tiny slits whenever the

whales surface. Other species living in troubled waters, like the South Asian river dolphin, have minuscule eyes with no lens. The diameter of their optic nerve is reduced, and the optic center in their brain has regressed to an extreme degree. The sense of sight does not prove all that useful in the muddy water they inhabit.

For a long time it was thought that dolphins saw correctly underwater but became myopic once they were out of it. In fact, their vision is much more effective than we imagined. Experiments with animals in captivity have proven that a bottlenose dolphin swimming beneath the surface can perfectly pinpoint an object five meters above its pool and hit the object every time it leaps. Thus, we know that dolphins can correct the variation in the refractive index caused by the change from water to air. Without this ability, they would systematically leap to one side of their targets. This supposes an ability to adjust their sight that is greatly superior to our own, according to a process whose details we still are far from mastering. All the same, we know that their corneas have an irregular surface, which probably facilitates the adjustment from water to air, their eye muscles permitting variations in the curve of their corneas. We also used to think that dolphins could not perceive colors, due to the rarity of cones on their retina, but experiments with dolphins in captivity have begun to show the contrary. In other words, we still "see darkly" what it is they see.

The spotted dolphins that came to meet us were decidedly very curious. One of them began to swim in circles around us. As I was observing him, I felt one of the girls give my hand a hard squeeze. I looked down through the water and discovered my intuition had not betrayed me.

Dolphins were around us everywhere! For a split second, I thought we had plunged into the midst of a living flood where the currents, instead of carrying us off, swept around our bodies without touching us. That morning, the water was very clear. We could see a good thirty meters down — and as far as the eye could see, there were animals. Dolphins by strata, by layer, and we were right in the thick of them! No doubt there were others, too, swimming in the depths beyond our view. As the horde swam beneath us, the water they displaced moved all over our skin, giving us little caresses. We could hear them as well, whistling and making "clicks." I think that the entire aggregation numbered over three hundred, but I confess to not having counted. I was content just to admire them. I remembered the mass exodus I had witnessed fourteen years earlier in the Bay of Biscay. How many times had I dreamed of finding myself in the midst of dolphins — and here I was! This time, it was not a question of a nomadic movement, since spotted dolphins in the region of the Azores stay in the same place all year long. We were witnessing some sort of daily assembly. Pods and larger groups were joining up again after having gone their separate ways, dispersing for a while to pursue their own activities.

Full of wonder and yet distraught, my two young companions searched out my gaze, looking for reassurance. I smiled at them and would have willingly given them a comforting pat, if they had only let go of my hands for a moment! This was totally out of the question. They weren't really frightened, but all these creatures swarming around made their hearts beat so quickly they hardly knew what to do. Bit by bit, they got hold of themselves, and I heard them talking through their snorkels. No doubt they were expressing their joy and amazement. What they said was of course incomprehensible, but the dolphins nearest to them reacted to every sound: moving briskly away, they veered off at a sharp angle or dived into the depths, trailing others behind them. It was as if the sounds the girls were making surprised them, causing them to scatter. But soon they were back again.

And then one of the girls cried out through her snorkel in a real fit of joy. In a split second, three hundred dolphins panicked and disappeared. We remained where we were, as if suspended in a vacuum. There they had been, so numerous they almost brushed against us, streaming by one after the other as if they were on a conveyor belt. Vanished! That was the last we saw of them for the entire day.

Later, on the deck of the *Fleur,* I remember secretly observing my two little divers. I can still see them now, sitting apart from the group, one up near the jib boom, the other at the foot of the companionway. Two misty-eyed dreamers. I know they were reliving those magical moments. Earlier on they had talked with their friends, gesturing animatedly as they recounted their extraordinary adventure. Still later that night, they would write and draw in their logs for hours, trying to capture their sensations and emotions. But at the moment I came upon them they were alone, lost in themselves and their emotions. I'm sure their hearts began to beat more quickly as they remembered the Atlantic spotted dolphins stirring up the ocean all around them. Such rare emotions abide in us for a lifetime.

The Ire of the Giant

There are two ways to ruin a scientific expedition: lose the funding or fall on bad luck. (But let's be honest: Bad luck is often due to bad planning. Luck doesn't fall from the sky—you've got to make your own.) The first of these problems has kept me, like other researchers, from successfully concluding projects. The second almost ruined one of my missions at sea. In 1983, during a project to determine the whale population in the North Atlantic, I made the mistake of taking on a teammate whom we quickly baptized "the chameleon," not because she knew how to adapt to her environment, but because she so persistently changed her colors from one moment to the next.

The objective of our monthlong expedition was to count baleen and sperm whales in a section of the Northeast Atlantic, in order to estimate their numbers in the high seas off the coast of Europe. At the time, Spain still had a fleet of whaling ships, but it was already preparing to join the ranks of countries that had declared themselves in favor of prohibiting whaling. With this goal in mind, the Spanish government was financing most of our operation. We had hired a tuna ship along with its Galician crew and set off from Vigo with a small group of Catalonian scientists, among whom our "chameleon" had hidden herself. I was the only French person aboard.

Such missions cost considerable sums of money—in our case, more than thirty thousand French francs, or roughly six thousand dollars at the 1983 rate of exchange, for every day at sea. This is public money destined for public benefit. We do not simply sail off into the blue, as some people like to imagine, but prepare our work down to the slightest detail. This involves years of study and calculations. Our particular mission was destined to furnish statistics for the International Whaling Commission, which was later to enact a statute permitting or prohibiting commercial whaling. Before boarding at Vigo, we had therefore devised an extremely precise way of counting whales and established a well-defined route. Thirty days at sea would give us the most cost-efficient mission. In other words, we had to be on watch at every instant, taking turns at the lookout post, binoculars in one hand and a chronometer in the other. As soon as we sighted a whale, we identified it and precisely noted the time, down to the very second. Then we entered this data on our portable computers. Our procedure necessitated a good deal of patience, because it is impossible to make a date with a whale, but it also required constant attention and a perfect knowledge of the species. And good reflexes, too. In order to function, it was better not to be subject to seasickness.

With very rare exceptions, anyone can become seasick. Even the saltiest sailors take some time to get their sea legs. During the first two or three days, we all do the best we can to battle the symptoms of nausea. As a general rule, it is important to eat well, drink copiously to combat dehydration, sleep, avoid needless fatigue and the odor of fuel, and be careful not to get sunburned. These were rules of good sense that our catastrophic teammate apparently had never heard of.

When she joined our expedition, our chameleon was still a student at a prestigious Spanish university. At twenty-four, she would soon be graduating, and I had no reason to doubt her competence. Fourteen years after the fact, I still am incapable of judging her aptitude, for she fell seasick the instant she stepped on board. She spent the initial night in agony in her bunk, at which time her face took on a sickly green tinge. She woke up in the morning as white as a sheet, but in good shape. So she went up to the forecastle wearing a swimsuit and sunglasses like a movie star, in order to work on her tan. Feeling a bit out of sorts myself, I weakly tried to dissuade her, but she refused to listen. After roasting herself for two hours, she ran, red as a lobster, to her cabin with her hand over her mouth. She came out again at sunset, completely livid—and went back to soak up the last rays of the sun, without eating or drinking a thing. Needless to say, she turned green again before nightfall and was sick as a dog.

These comings and goings would have remained on the level of pure anecdote if the chameleon had not been so hardheaded. The next day, she began the whole thing over again! And nothing could change her mind—neither the supplications of the other student researchers on the ship, nor the advice of the crew, nor my own insistence. While the rest of us were doing everything we could to avoid the curse of seasickness on the first few days of the voyage, she made a point of doing just the opposite. Not only did she continue in the same vein, she doubled the sun and halved her consumption of food and water. Day after day, she was white at morning, red at noon, and green at night. This went on for a whole week, until we finally had to turn around and go back to Vigo, where our chameleon was carried away on a stretcher and hospitalized for dehydration.

I can't help adding a parting touch—one without consequences for anyone but me, who shared the chameleon's cabin. Night after night, in a space of six square meters, I put up with her complaints, her moans and groans, and the despair of the worst of her crisis—and all week long, she vomited in my boots!

The mission might well have ended right then and there because of a single mule-headed, irresponsible person. Luckily, the program was not canceled and we were able to obtain new funding that enabled us to head back out on the course we had traced through the Bay of Biscay out to the open sea.

At one point, our route took us along the edge of the continental shelf. Crews on ocean liners and racing yachts know this area well because of the high risk of running into particularly difficult conditions. Along the shelf line, where the bottom of the ocean floor suddenly rises up from a thousand meters to barely two hundred deep, enormous swells create a very dangerous sea. The area is also biologically rich, and always abounding in fish—just the kind of place that whales go looking for.

For fifteen days, we barely saw a single whale. I can think of nothing more wearisome than spending the entire day at a lookout post with my eyes glued to binoculars, staring at an empty sea. For a couple of hours it is beautiful, but on an expedition meant to gather statistics, it is above all frustrating, annoying, and draining. Little by little, this watching and waiting also creates a feeling of guilt that is very hard to shake. Even though the absence of whales was not a failure for us, but simply a negative observation, we had the impression of wasting time and money. Why had we ever got involved in this business?

Although we, the empty-handed researchers, were feeling quite upset, our crew of Spanish sailors couldn't have been happier. Working under the direction of our skipper, Manuel, they fished for tuna all day long. They caught enough to fill up the entire ship. The hold was overflowing with it, and so were the kitchen, the gangways, and every nook and cranny where shade could be found on deck. They were stashing tuna everywhere—even in the cabins! "Bonito! Bonito!" Manuel's men cried out ten times a day—when I desperately wanted to hear them shout *"Ballena! Ballena!"*— whales! The lines were cast, and the tuna landed at our feet. There were dozens and dozens of them. The cook, giddy with such abundance, frenetically tried to keep up. There was no end to the dishes he came up with—tuna in olive oil, tuna and tomatoes, tuna *à la plancha,* tuna soup—tuna, tuna, tuna, morning, noon, and night. We ate so much tuna we got indigestion. We even dreamed about it. For ten whole years after this expedition, I couldn't eat tuna; even the tiniest flake in a *salade niçoise* was enough to make me shudder.

And finally, one morning three hundred kilometers at sea off the coast of France, we heard—

"There she blows!"

We ran to our observation posts. The watchman was on
his feet, his arm outstretched, pointing to the port side horizon. I turned with my binoculars just in time to glimpse a
second plume of spray.

"Sperm whales!"

We all cried out in unison. They had surfaced more than
a kilometer away, but the jet of this largest of the tooth
whales is immediately identifiable. The cloud of mist surges
out at a slant to the left, about forty-five degrees from the
water's surface, while that of a baleen whale goes more or
less straight up to the sky. Before asking our captain to head
toward them, one of our teammates noted down our exact
position, consulting the GPS. On these special missions, the
data we collect are of value only if we follow a very precise
route. If we zigzag, or worse, go around in circles, no reliable information results from our observations. Once the
observation is finished, if we have deviated from course,
we have to turn around again and go back to where we
branched off. We always return to our initial route.

This particular day, we reduced our speed and neared
the two whales we had located, a calf and its mother. In
adult sperm whales, sexual dimorphism is so pronounced
that it is easy to identify the chief male in any harem. The
calves are about four meters long at birth. While female
adults reach a length of twelve meters and a weight of about
fifteen tons, males sometimes surpass sixteen meters and
can weigh up to forty-five tons. The silhouette of a sperm
whale is certainly the most readily recognizable of all
marine mammals, even though it has no fin on its back.
Instead, a series of bumps runs along the length of its back

down to the stem of its tail. The first of these, which is often triangularly shaped, is larger than the rest. The skin on the whale's back and sides is wrinkled, varying in color from brown to gray. The blowhole, shaped like an S, is situated on the left front side of its enormous head, thus determining the particular angle of its jet. The head itself, shaped like a parallelogram, measures a third of the entire length of the body.

This was the first time I had ever had the chance to see sperm whales, and I remember being struck by the enormous sense of power they emanated. They had an apparent invincibility, reinforced by an impression of calmness. All they had to do was spout to reveal their colossal force. Like baleen whales, sperm whales move effortlessly. An imperceptible movement of their tails propels them forward, an ease that undoubtedly contributed to their reputation as supernatural monsters.

We put our motor in neutral about thirty meters away from the mother and her calf and continued to search the sea, looking for other individuals. I doubted that these two were the only ones in the area. While large males travel alone in the polar regions, sperm whales in temperate zones move together in groups. It is possible to encounter groups of young males or adult females accompanied by their young. Most often, we come across a harem carefully guarded by an enormous male, who has conquered the females in tremendous battles. In coastal waters, such harems can number up to forty whales, but in the open sea they are often one-forth that number.

I hadn't been mistaken. We had been waiting in place,

gently rocking from side to side, for less than fifteen minutes when the rest of the pod surfaced. There were six of
them including the patriarch, a gargantuan creature worthy
of Moby Dick, with the exception of his color. He was a
dark gray-blue, almost black, and covered in scars from the
tip of his jaw down to the middle of his body—testaments
to glorious combat with giant squid in the total darkness of
the ocean's depths. He had surfaced to the side of his harem
but came up to us with just a few strokes of his tail and positioned himself between the ship and his females.

As soon as I saw him coming so close, I told the captain
to start up again and slowly move off. Surprised, Manuel
complied, but he murmured something under his breath to
the effect that we were not in danger. At the time, I was not
so sure of myself. Today, I would insist on backing up without hesitation, because the alpha male was sending us a very
clear message: the moment he stopped beside the ship, he
half-opened his mouth. And when a predator shows you his
teeth, he's not smiling—he's warning you that he's armed to
kill.

This time, we stayed near the whales. I hadn't been able
to persuade the crew to leave so quickly, and I felt a furious
desire to continue watching them myself. Along with blue
whales, sperm whales are the most fabulous creatures I
have ever had the good fortune to approach. It is almost
impossible to imagine that life can take such strangely
disproportionate dimensions. We can accept the most incredible metabolisms in insects and bacteria, but where
mammals are concerned we feel compelled to refuse the
facts. They are too much like us, and at the same time we
are still ignorant of too many things about them.

The way sperm whales dive, for instance—their most common activity—remains a puzzle, even if we regularly discover physiological particularities that permit us partially to explain their performances. We know, for example, that their muscles can absorb up to 50 percent of the oxygen they take in, which is twice the capacity of land mammals. It is probable that their spermaceti, which occupies a large portion of their head, also helps them to dive. The nasal cavities and sinuses traversing the spermaceti presumably permit them to regulate the temperature of this oily substance, which remains at twenty-nine degrees Celsius in the liquid state. When a sperm whale passes from warm surface waters to the colder depths, the oil constituting the melon is chilled. It follows that the spermaceti solidifies, retracts, and increases the density of the head, which helps the whale to descend. When the whale surfaces, the blood flow increases in the capillaries of its head, heating up the fatty acids. The resulting increase in buoyancy permits the tired animal to surface more easily.

For a long time, we thought whales could only descend to a depth of twelve hundred meters, because that is where we had found them stuck under transatlantic telephone cables. That was already phenomenally deep, but today our ultraperformance sonar has shown us that sperm whales attain a depth of three thousand meters with incredible speed, traveling at one hundred seventy meters a minute. The pressure should permanently crush them, yet they resist perfectly well, and furthermore take time to hunt in the darkness of the abyss. They stay down without breathing for an hour or more and surface at a rate of one hundred forty meters a minute. This wonder has never been observed, and remains one of our primary challenges. In France, specialized laboratories like Comex are attempting to observe how whales feed on the ocean floor. In theory, it should suffice to fix a miniature camera on top of a sperm whale's head, but the camera would also have to resist the pressure, and be able to register images in total darkness. Then, the camera would also have to be operated by remote control when the whale is underwater, and, above all, we would have to be able to get it back when the animal surfaces again.

We have not yet figured out the solutions to these problems, but a *National Geographic* team has been working on them. Sea lions are also capable of diving deeply, and researchers are trying to equip them so they can be used to film the whales. But first, it is necessary to train the sea lions to turn their heads on command to watch the "movie stars!" There is plenty of work ahead of us yet if we hope to come up with convincing information. In fact, the whole undertaking constitutes a tremendous field of investigation for biologists, technicians, and gadget-making geniuses. Fortunately, no one has yet found a means of capturing a sperm whale for purposes of study and keeping it alive in a swimming pool three thousand meters deep by tossing it a mere two hundred kilos of giant squid a day!

I was struck with wonder to see these living mountains advancing before my eyes, and I confess to forgetting my fears after a few minutes in their company. But when the patriarch dived, I again was flooded with anxiety. He seemed agitated after watching us circle his females for the past half hour. Or was it just me, projecting my uneasiness on him? I looked around. The crew seemed indifferent, and my

teammates were still enthralled with the spectacle of five female whales gathered in a single group.

Then, suddenly, the ocean exploded. The male hurtled
up from the deep, breaking the surface thirty meters from
the boat. He rose almost vertically, leaping entirely from the
water with an open mouth, displaying teeth fifteen centimeters long, then came down on his back. Forty tons of
muscle, bone, and blubber slammed into the water. The
punch of a giant's fist, inciting a mini-tidal wave. Our
twenty-eight-meters long tuna boat danced like a cork.
We were lucky no one was thrown overboard.

It was our second warning, and this time we got the message: we were in the way. In the blink of an eye, the lookout
abandoned his post and Manuel leapt to the controls. We
left without further ado.

I don't know why the male was angry, but I suppose we
came along and annoyed him at the wrong time. If one of
their own is wounded or in trouble, sperm whales often
form a "daisy," grouping in a circle around the individual
they want to protect and pressing their foreheads against it.
In whaling days, this solidarity was their ruin. I did not
observe this sort of behavior, but the male would not have
displayed immediate hostility without a reason. One of
their members may have been ill, or there may have been a
young calf, and so our presence was possibly interpreted as
a threat. If our boat had been smaller, he might have leapt a
second time, attacking us at the risk of his own life, just as
his ancestors attacked the whalers who harassed them, reduc-
ing their harpoon boats to matchsticks. Better to flee: pro-
voking the ire of giants was not part of our mission.

We retraced our path and took up our initial route again. For four days running, we came across fin whales and numerous pods of dolphins, but no sperm whales. Our observations were going well, but something had changed on board the ship: Manuel's men weren't fishing anymore. Far be it from me to complain—I was hoping that they, in turn, were sick of eating tuna at every meal. But alas, I was mistaken. The fifth day, with French fishing boats all around us, Tony, the boatswain, asked me with embarrassment if we could have a private talk.

"We've got a problem," said Tony.

We often spoke English on this strange ship, although there was not an Anglo-Saxon aboard. The crew was Galician, the researchers Catalan, and speaking Castilian was out of the question. Tony addressed me in a singsong, rudimentary English that usually greatly amused me—but not this time.

"I hear that you're part Breton," said Tony. "The fishermen around here are also from Brittany . . ."

True, by blood I am half Breton, but by adoption I am even more thoroughly so. My parents owned a house near Camaret where we spent all our family vacations. Later, when I was a student at Brest, I lived on the Crozon Peninsula. Tony continued:

"Would you mind talking to some other Bretons to ask them something?"

"Not at all. What do you want from them?"

"Some lures."

"To go fishing? You mean to tell me that you're not fishing tuna anymore because you've run out of bait? Is that it?"

Tony nodded his head yes.

"And you want me to ask them to give you some of theirs?"

Again, the boatswain agreed. I was trapped. The very idea that our deck—and my plate—would be heaped with tuna again was enough to nauseate me. But if I refused, the crew would hold it against me and our expedition would be affected by bad feelings. On the other hand, the French and Spanish fishing fleets were heavy, even brutal, competitors; if I managed to get in the good graces of the French, I was certain our crew would do anything I wanted. Except stop serving me tuna—it was just too much to expect them to understand that I was sick of it.

"OK, Tony, come with me over to the radio."

I had only one hope left: that the Frenchmen would refuse to give me the lures. The owner of the first boat I contacted on the radio was a guy from Guilvinec. I had no sooner introduced myself than he cried out with a strong local accent, using the familiar "tu":

"Anne Collet! Hey, you're from Camaret!"

He had navigated the harbor at Brest and knew all about the sailboat races I'd been in. He gave me the lures without hesitation, sealing the bait in a plastic keg that our Galician fishermen brought in on the end of a boat hook. French lures are different from the ones the Spanish use. Initially perplexed, our boatswain finally declared that if Bretons managed to catch tuna with such funny-looking stuff, he'd damn well be able to do it too. Thanks to me, we soon had tuna galore again, on the menu morning, noon, and night. I'm still mad at myself.

Of course, all expeditions to count whales at sea are
not so colorful. They are not always punctuated by seasick
chameleons, furiously fishing Galicians, and sperm whales
leaping to the sky. This particular mission was both unique
and useful: three years later, thanks in part to our work in
the Bay of Biscay, and to many other similar missions, the
massacre of whales for commercial purposes was finally
forbidden.

A Morning Dip with Moby Dick

The shaft of the harpoon he was holding in his fist looked no larger than the handle of a pickax—but appearances are deceiving. This was the hand of a hunter, large, callused, and thick, and his weapon had not been carved for delicate fingers. Older than seventy, he was still robust. White hair, a face deeply furrowed by a lifetime of salt and sun, old familiar aches in his back and shoulders, no doubt, poor eyesight—but it was clear that retirement had barely diminished the physical stamina he had acquired on the stem of a whaling ship.

The hunter brandished his harpoon for us, miming a gesture centuries old: "Like this!" His weapon never left his hand, but we divined the throw had been vigorous, that the steel could fly ten meters and pierce a sperm whale's side. How many had he killed? A few dozen, and some of them giants, enormous males next to which the whaleboat looked quite fragile. Every time he met a sperm whale face to face, the old hunter had risked his life, as did all of his companions, friends, and brothers. Some of them never came back to the island alive. With one swat of its tail, a single leap, a whale crazed from the iron in its flesh could reduce any whaler in the Azores to matchsticks.

Like a knight of old at a castle door, the hunter stood at attention in front of his house on Pico, his weapon placed at his feet. He began to tell us stories. His stories. Tales of fury, blood, and sea fog, tales of death. He enumerated the "benefits" of his profession. Whale oil was used to make soap, margarine, nitroglycerine, and paint, and was employed in the tanning of hides. Spermaceti produced candles, polishing cloths, crayons, chalk, food wrapping, lipstick, eye shadow, shampoo. Seated around him in a circle, the children from the *Fleur de Lampaul* couldn't believe their ears. This impressive-looking old man had been introduced as a hero, and here he turned out to be a whale killer. And he didn't feel one bit guilty!

In 1991, in the mind of a thirteen-year-old, it had to be one or the other—hero *or* whale killer. Our children are born in an ecologically conscious age and are inculcated, at the very least, with a theoretical respect for nature. Whales and dolphins are symbols enshrined in their imagination. Those who kill them or have done so in the past are barbarians, blasphemers against life, monsters. And yet, the old man before them, with his strong hands, square shoulders, and deep voice, was anything but an assassin. The children sensed this. They were discovering that received ideas and gross generalities are rarely good ideas, right ideas. They were discovering that it is possible to have killed dozens of superb creatures and still be a good man.

Obviously, the old harpooner from the Azores standing before them had never commanded a factory trawler, a gigantic meat grinder for whales. Our hunter from Pico stood in the bow of an open harpoon boat ten meters long,

powered only by oar. He lifted his lance against an animal a
thousand times larger and stronger than himself. His hands
never held a harpoon launcher to fire weapons with explo-
sive heads. For him, the hunt was a battle. And once he had
pierced the side of a whale, he engaged in face-to-face combat until the whale was dead. Then the men towed the whale
home, dragging it with the help of a winch onto a slipway
before cutting it up, taking out its spermaceti, and removing
its blubber as if peeling a banana. All these were melted
down and sold in Europe.

This kind of hunting did not last long: barely more than
a hundred years. Sperm whale hunting started in the Azores
in the mid-nineteenth century, when rorquals and hump-
backs began to become scarce. Industries of every sort were
crying for oil. Baleen whales had already been systematically
chased for centuries. On Spitsbergen, the Dutch had even
founded "Blubbertown," a colony with a population of eighteen thousand dedicated to the whale-butchering industry.
By the time the Portuguese began to hunt sperm whales in
the Azores much later, chasing baleen whales had long since
turned into a massacre. Precision navigation instruments,
reliable weather predictions, and new technologies permitted fleets of whaling ships to track down cetaceans on an
enormous scale in every ocean on the planet. Distant expeditions multiplied, transforming the Southern Hemisphere
into the whaler's preferred hunting ground.

Sailors from the Azores never saw these far horizons
nor used these new techniques. As recently as thirty years
ago, harpooning remained a traditional skill: whaleboats
were equipped with nothing more than motors—the only

"progress" the hunters ever accepted. Their exploits live in human memory, but their catch was minimal in relation to the butchery in other places, especially in the Southern seas. They killed no more than a dozen whales a year, and never endangered the species. Elsewhere it was different, and the blood flowed freely. From 1956 to 1965, close to 404,000 baleen whales and over 228,000 sperm whales were slaughtered throughout the world. In 1964 alone, more than 29,000 sperm whales paid the cost of human greed, greed so bloodthirsty that it endangered the biological equilibrium of the entire planet.

The old harpooner from the Azores had probably never read these figures anywhere or, if he knew them, they meant nothing to him. He stood before the children from the *Fleur de Lampaul*, explaining that he still did not understand why it was that one morning in 1975 he'd been obliged to stop chasing sperm whales. Hunting was dangerous, it was noble.

Voyages on the *Fleur* are about the school of life—adventure is only a pretext. The children succeeded in listening to the old whale killer, in really hearing what he had to say. They learned a good lesson before going hunting themselves—with empty hands.

Two days after this conversation, the *Fleur* took to the sea again. We were sailing in the company of another vessel equipped for scientific missions, the *Song of the Whales*, skippered by Jonathan Gordon. Smaller than the *Fleur*, the *Song* had for years been a base for studying sperm whales, crisscrossing the waters of the Azores. Jonathan's research relies on acoustic techniques, using directional underwater microphones, receivers, and specially conceived computer programs to locate, identify, follow, and rejoin the animals he studies. From year to year, the *Song* has become a veritable floating laboratory full of monitors, keyboards, computers, and all kinds of sophisticated electronic devices. The bunks, the kitchen, the cupboards all are full of them. Jonathan was kind enough to take our apprentices on board and initiate them into his work.

It took us a dozen hours, one whole night of navigation, to locate the animals: seven sperm whales in all, five adult females with two calves. This time, we planned on joining up with them in the Zodiac, an inflatable dinghy with an outboard motor.

As the Zodiac leapt from crest to crest on the waves, nearing the whales' black backs, I was certain that my young companions were still thinking about the old harpooner from Pico. Their minds were also full of scenes from *Moby Dick*, which we had read aloud the night before in the mess room:

> Suddenly the waters around them slowly swelled in broad circles; then quickly upheaved, as if sideways sliding from a submerged berg of ice, swiftly rising to the surface. A low rumbling sound was heard; a subterraneous hum; and then all held their breaths; as bedraggled with trailing ropes, and harpoons, and lances, a vast form shot lengthwise, but obliquely from the sea. Shrouded in a thin drooping veil of mist, it hovered for a moment in the rainbowed air; and then fell swamping back into the deep. Crushed thirty feet upwards, the waters flashed for an instant like heaps of fountains, then brokenly sank in a shower of flakes, leaving the circling surface creamed like new milk round the marble trunk of the whale.

These few resplendent sentences capture the entire legend of the sperm whale.

Leaving the deck of a solid twenty-meter vessel like the *Fleur*, heading toward the whales on a little craft as low in the water as a harpoon boat, we relived the emotions Melville discovered in whalers from Nantucket and New Bedford. Sperm whales are literally terrifying, like no other creature on earth. When "the waters around them slowly swelled in broad circles," we held our breath and had to master a sense of rising panic. The appearance of the largest baleen whales, by contrast, does not send shivers down our spines, maybe because we consider them "grazers" of krill rather than predators. But sperm whales are armed with teeth and an intelligence that permits them to chase down prey—in other words, to follow, hunt, and fight with them, and seize them for the kill. Even if this potential is not revealed at first sight, we sense it instinctively, just as we know we're up against something bigger than we are.

It was not by chance that the voyage of the *Fleur* led us to this group of whales. I, too, had questions to ask the old harpooner at Pico, and he willingly divulged some of his secrets, which now were no longer of use to him. We were sure to find whales in the Azores, where they come every spring and leave at the end of autumn, but I needed him to indicate a precise area. The "nurseries" made up of females and calves spend most of their time in tropical and subtropical waters, while the males travel much farther, ranging from the equator to the polar seas. Just the year before, a sperm whale with a harpoon from the Azores in his side had been captured in Iceland. Their migration north takes place in summer, according to complex rhythms that change with the whale's age. At first, the young males remain with the females, but as they become older, they break up into groups. Later still, when they are old, they often live alone most of the year.

Although we understand these mechanisms better and better now, they eluded us for many years, because we thought the sperm whales' migration patterns resembled those of baleen whales. We were on the wrong track, and from here on out it will be a long process to refine our findings to the point of certitude. In any case, we do know that the nurseries stay together and are joined by the males during periods of reproduction. At this time, the males do battle, banging heads and availing themselves of their teeth to conquer their harems. They do not reclaim the same group of females year after year, but go from one to the other, faithful for a single mating season. Males continue to grow throughout their lives, which average about seventy years, so the older they are, the bigger they become. Victory in these titanic battles often goes to enormous patriarchs, who sometimes win with the help of the females. Frequently, the cost is a broken jaw.

No male accompanied the females we were now approaching. Perhaps he had already gone north, or had gone for a dive. When we were fifty meters away from the animals, I asked that the motor be cut. One adult would stay in the boat, ready to help, while two children and I were in the water. In cases like ours, the rules of safety are simple but strict: no loud noises, no sudden movements, no frenetic paddling with the flippers, stay with the group, and do not leave the whales' field of vision, for their binocular eyesight is poor and they cannot turn their heads. We should not oblige our hosts to turn around in order to see us. We are in their home, they have not invited us, and we should comport ourselves like guests who have unexpectedly stopped off for a visit. I looked the whales over a final time.

"It's OK, they're calm. Let's go."

The children seemed uneasy, and hesitated. They were probably remembering the old harpooner's stories, or our reading of *Moby Dick.*

"How do you know they're going to stay calm?"

It was imperative that I reassure them; otherwise they ran the risk of frightening the animals in spite of themselves. I talked to them about the peaceful attitude in the pod, the slowness of their movements, the fact that our presence seemed not at all to bother the females, the curiosity of the calves. But in fact, I had no rational proof to give them. It was all intuitive. In my deepest self, I was convinced there was no risk. A predator always announces its intentions. It's all a question of recognizing the signals. In fact, it is necessary to be ready to beat a retreat at the least sign of hostility or fear. I am sure that no whale would ever choose to attack a human in the open sea. In their element, they have no, or very few, predators, and they know they can put a quick stop to any unpleasant situation—they dive, and no one can follow.

As a general rule, an animal that can run away from danger without endangering its own immediate or future survival—if it is not defending its territory, for example—will choose this solution rather than a fight. A confrontation is riskier—someone could get hurt! But people have difficulty sharing my convictions when they've already got their flippers on and creatures weighing ten or fifteen tons are bobbing around them within hearing range. Finally, the attraction of the whales themselves conquered my young acolytes' anxiety, and we let ourselves into the water.

This time, Guillaume and Pierre, both twelve or thirteen, accompanied me. Usually these two were ready for anything, always the first to climb the shrouds, the first to high dive off the end of the jib boom. But on this day, they seemed to shiver with timidity. They were swimming so close to me I had trouble moving my arms. To help them relax, since the water was very clear and I knew they were good divers, I suggested we observe the whales from three or four meters beneath the surface. They agreed, and we dived like ducks, without a sound.

The whales were having a chat! True, we couldn't hear them as well as we had that morning, when we passed around the headset to the hydrophone. Our ears are not made to hear underwater. Just as images are blurry when we look through water, so too our ears perceive only a limited span of sound frequencies under the surface. Nevertheless, we heard some clicking and clacking, a moaning sound like stifled cries, then noises that sounded like a squeaky door opening on poorly oiled hinges. The concert lasted only a few seconds. We went back up for air, but when we dived a second time, they had stopped. My companions were flabbergasted.

"You think they're talking to each other?"

"They're communicating. We so rarely hear them that

for a long time we thought they were mute. For the most part, we've only heard the cries the males make when they are fighting."

"And you think they can tell each other stuff—stuff about us?"

I would have had trouble answering that one. I made do with a grimace to show I didn't know. The sight of the five females with their two calves was magical. Swimming around us in circles, from time to time they dipped about ten meters below the surface, then came back up and released a jet of vapor. We had the impression that the mothers and aunts were dancing a ballet, allowing their young ones to turn and play all around them. They didn't seem worried about us in the least. This was so much so that one of my divers started worrying himself.

"What if they haven't even seen us? What will they do when they realize we're here?"

"Don't worry, they've seen us. And even if they haven't, they've heard and smelled us, too. Well, actually, they've 'tasted' us."

I'd made a big mistake. The whales could not "smell" us underwater, because their blowhole is hermetically sealed. But given the situation, the word *taste* was out of place because it suggested they might want to eat us. There was no time to explain, but I promised to do so once we were back on the *Fleur.*

In point of fact, sperm whales detect changes in the salinity of water through taste buds distributed throughout their mouths. This mode of detection is a survival mechanism on which they depend to discover food and potential mates. They "smell" at a distance the chemical substances their prey emit, although they do this poorly, since their olfactory nerves and lobes have all but disappeared. They taste with much more subtlety anything that comes in the immediate vicinity of their mouths, and they analyze molecules detectable in water long after they have been dissolved. Tooth whales no longer have the nasal mucus cells their land mammal ancestors once possessed, for these would no longer be useful. Their blowhole is hermetically sealed underwater, and it only opens briefly when they surface. By contrast, baleen whales, which have no sonar, seem to have a better sense of smell and taste than sperm whales do. They use these senses to locate the banks of krill they devour.

But once again, none of this information is set in stone. Scientists have recently discovered that several species of tooth whales have, at the base of their tongue, buds and pores containing the chemically receptive cells that create the sense of taste. The dolphins concerned are thus capable of distinguishing a great number of chemical substances dissolved in the water and can discern the difference among sweet, sour, bitter, and salty. In captivity, they immediately refuse any mackerel whose freshness leaves something to be desired. So I wasn't lying when I said that whales "taste" people who approach them in the water. But even more, they use their supersonar to locate us by sound.

We continued our cautious approach to the whales, then stopped at a respectable distance. The animals continued their dance with as much suppleness and power as ever, and I was convinced their attitude toward us would remain the same as long as we did not cross the invisible line surrounding their circle of safety. They show no fear of humans, and whatever fear they might possibly feel must be comparable

to the feelings a spider on a table inspires in us. When it
runs away we feel nothing, unless it is sometimes revulsion.
But if it gets disoriented, suddenly turns around, and scam-
pers toward us on its long hairy legs, we may be gripped by
irrational fear. One swat, and that's the end of the spider.

Our sense of vocation hardly included being conked
with the tail of a sperm whale. Respecting what I judged
to be the perimeter of their safety zone, we swam either at
the surface or a few meters under it. The two boys began to
relax, and the worry in their eyes gave place to wonderment.
Again, I asked myself who was observing whom: we had
searched the whales out in order to contemplate them; they
allowed us to approach in order to get a closer look at us.

One of the calves seemed particularly attached to its
mother's "apron strings." Playing a sort of miming game,
it copied the female's every movement so well that at times
we seemed to be watching a miniature image reflected in a
mirror, reduced to a half-scale model. Then, suddenly, the
mother half-opened her mouth, less than fifteen meters
away from us. My companions froze instantly, then slowly
mounted to the surface, rising like two balloons. I'd told
them about the experience with sperm whales I'd had on my
counting expedition on the tuna boat, and they remembered
the motto of the story: "When a predator shows its teeth,
it's rarely smiling." It was a good reaction on their part, even
if this time the female did not manifest any sign of aggressiveness. Her open mouth must rather have been a signal to
her calf. That said, she had all the same just swung open
a narrow jaw two meters long, garnished with more than
forty conical teeth, each weighing a good kilo.

Whales' teeth have given rise to the wildest fantasies.

Someone put forth the hypothesis that deep in the abyss their whiteness attracts giant squid, which precipitate themselves toward the whales like sailors rushing into the arms of sirens, only to be ground up into shreds. But lo and behold, the squid found in whales' stomachs are not ground up, but whole: their predators have not taken the time to chew their food. Moreover, they would be hard put to do so, since only the lower half of their fabled jaws has teeth. The upper jaw has tooth sockets, holes that lodge the lower teeth when the giant closes its mouth. To be more precise, their upper jaw is equipped with a few vestigial teeth that never pierce the gum. Sperm whales consume 3 to 4 percent of their weight in food every day. And yet, the teeth of the oldest individuals are worn down and blunted. They must be grinding against something, but we have yet to learn what it is.

Cetaceans have extravagant dentition. Those that feed on squid have a reduced set of teeth; this is the case for pilot whales, pygmy sperm whales, dwarf sperm whales, and Risso's dolphins. Beaked whales, which are also squid feeders, have only two teeth, planted in their lower jaw. But these must not be terribly useful, for in the females they often don't even break the gum. And yet the females nourish themselves every bit as easily as the males. The male narwhal has developed a single tooth shaped like a cabled sword. Several times, I have discovered common dolphins washed up on the beach without any teeth at all, when ordinarily they have 160 of them. They were victims of infections or osteoporosis, and their gums were completely healed over. They weighed just as much as their fellow dolphins, which proves that their toothless gums did not keep them from eating. In the end, their impressive teeth really aren't all that much use to them.

At most, they use them to grip the livelier fish as they try to escape, twisting themselves every which way—and we are not even sure about this. It seems that dolphins catch their prey by suction. They rush in, hit them with their snouts to stun them a bit, then suck them in, always headfirst, swallowing in the direction of the scales.

Obviously, our mother whale with the open mouth did not confuse us with squid wearing flippers, and we arrived safe and sound back at the boat. Although the adventure was at an end for my teammates, this was not the case for me. I had no idea if we would be so lucky the next day, and I preferred to take advantage of the pod's hospitality to bring the other children out to meet them. As a result, I remained in the water that morning for over three hours.

The Atlantic Ocean in the region of the Azores is not exactly a Caribbean beach. Teeth chattering, I came on board the *Fleur* chilled to the bone and utterly exhausted. But beyond the strict observation of animals in their natural environment, the pleasure I experienced in conducting the children into the giants' company was well worth the massive loss of calories. I never experience this feeling of harmony when I approach whales with adults.

I am convinced that sperm whales, like all mammals, understand when they are dealing with our "young," our children, and that it isn't a question of size or morphology. Are they able to perceive innocence and spontaneity? They instinctively understand that the beings before them are not completely formed, that they are still in the process of becoming. As a general rule, the young of the animal world are not yet physically and mentally equipped to inflict harm.

This differentiates the stage of childhood from adulthood. People are the same way: if we see a wolf we feel wary, to say the least—but we are attracted by its cubs and want to pet them. In any case, fear does not determine our reaction. And where there is no fear there is no aggression, except if one party is fundamentally the prey of the other. I am convinced that cetaceans have kept this instinctive propensity.

The feeling of security I experience when I dive with children reveals the bonds uniting us to cetaceans. We share a common ancestor, and probably many more aspects than we imagine. Most of the legends about friendship between a dolphin and a human emphasize the youth of the "schoolboy" or the "little sailor." This bond is magnified in the myth of the dolphin and the beautiful boy from Iassos who love each other and always swim together. One day, the boy takes a hard dive, landing against the dolphin's back and striking his stomach on the dorsal fin, which happens to be pointing upward. Pierced through the navel, the boy dies, and the dolphin, crazed with grief, dies of love. They are buried in the same tomb, which becomes a shrine for worshiping the god Eros.

There is something marvelous in this communion, all the more so in that children themselves are unconscious of it. They remain receptive and curious, lost in their joy. It is very moving to see adolescents swept away by their interests, especially as my functions otherwise oblige me to listen to students who are at a loss, who are incapable of saying precisely what it is they want to do, what it is they like or admire. They have no desires, no passions. This is because they have never been given the opportunity to experiment on their own in areas that interest them. They end up convincing themselves that they are interested in nothing, that they are good-for-nothings themselves.

By nature somewhat a perfectionist, I am rarely totally satisfied by my acts. But I feel true contentment whenever I recall diving with our interns from the *Fleur de Lampaul* because I feel that I helped awaken the kind of passionate interest that asks no more than the chance to express itself. I am sure they have benefited from diving with dolphins and whales, and maybe they have also learned a lesson: when you really want to do something, don't hesitate—figure out a way, and do it!

Adventures on Spitsbergen

Seventy-eight degrees north, nearly eight hundred kilometers from the northernmost tip of Europe: snow
and ice everywhere. And yet nothing is white. The ground,
the sea, the glaciers, the sky—everything is blue, gray, gray-
blue, blue-marine, emerald green, shading into warm colors,
from golden yellow to deep red, as the sun approaches the
horizon. Nothing is "really" white. The air is absolutely
pure. I inhale and feel 200 percent alive. Polar regions fascinate me, and on Spitsbergen I feel at home.

The summer expedition we organized in the Norwegian
archipelago in 1989 primarily brought together ornitholo-
gists seeking to count new colonies of birds: to take a census of northern fulmars, common kittiwakes, black and
common guillemots, little auks, and other species. As for
me, I had the additional objective of observing belugas—
curious, peaceful cetaceans, dolphins actually—which are
sometimes called "white whales." I also wanted to drink
in the source of the far north. Ever since my first trip to
northern Canada, where I was occupied with problems related to the overpopulation of seals, I've been unable to stay
away from frozen lands for very long. The Arctic and the

Antarctic passionately interest me. I manage to resist their attraction for a few months or a year, but rarely longer. One morning at last, the occasion presents itself for an escapade on a polar ice cap—and I'm off.

But a monthlong stay on Spitsbergen, the principal island in the Svalbard archipelago, cannot be improvised. A tourist cruise company chartering steamers in the region had assisted us by having one of their ships drop off our five hundred kilos of equipment in a hut at the end of the world. We were to arrive later, after a long journey that took us from Paris to Oslo, then on to Tromsö and Longyearbyen, the largest "city" on the island. As our budget prohibited us from taking a helicopter, we plied the coast from there on a small steamship up to Ny-Alesund, the northernmost community in the world. This is closer to the North Pole than Thule in Greenland, which Jean Malaurie, the famous French ethnologist, immortalized in his writings on civilizations of the far north.

Our wooden hut—fifty square meters without heat that served us as a warehouse—was rented by the year and cost a small fortune. Everything in the polar regions is atrociously expensive, because everything is imported. Because the French observation base installed on the island was neither very welcoming nor very practical for the fieldwork we wanted to accomplish, we had no solution other than this wooden hut lost on the ice. In fact, it was less a true lodging than a temperamental freezer where we stored our necessities from one season to the next. We were camped out at the edge of the shore, some hundred meters from the village. On the hottest summer day, the thermometer rose to five degrees Celsius, and in winter it easily went down to just below minus forty degrees Celsius. These extremes of temperature make it hard for foodstuffs to survive, even sacks of rice and pasta. We nevertheless had to bring everything to Spitsbergen and stock it there, for local prices are prohibitive—five to six times higher than in France, even for the most basic goods.

It took us four days to inventory our equipment: fresh food, replacement parts brought from France, and then the tin trunks, veritable caves of Ali Baba, that we had left behind the season before. My log contains sixteen pages of lists worthy of an inventory à la poet Jacques Prévert. (Hey! Packages of noodles, and they're only six years old. Yum! Chocolate bars, frozen, thawed, and refrozen probably twenty times in three years. Terrific! A piece from a motor that no one can identify.) We discovered these "treasures," sorted them, then classified them as "trek out," "trek back," and "expedition barrels" (numbered from one to nine), not to mention the "survival barrels" we hoped not to use. Spread out on the ice, our food, instruments, equipment, and three inflatable dinghies with their outboard motors covered more than a hundred square meters—and there were only six of us. Nothing is simple or easy in these regions; accumulation and bulk are the rule. The least oversight sometimes costs very dearly, and a little problem can rapidly turn into a disaster.

For reasons of security, the Norwegian authorities no longer allow people on shore in the archipelago unless they bring a rifle. The season before we arrived, three Danish scientists had come south to work in the same regions we were going to cover. Peaceful, gentle people, they did not want to carry guns. One morning, a polar bear intruded on their camp. He approached with a determined step, wagging his head from left to right, tracking the scent of humans, his muzzle pressed against the ice. Without guns, it was impossible for the Danish to chase away, let alone kill, the enormous flat-footed beast attacking them. One of the men was carried a few meters away and devoured before the eyes of his helpless companions. An exceptional drama, of course, but also a predictable one, since it is known that approximately 5 percent of polar bears will not hesitate to treat humans as ordinary prey.

Bears are not the only danger: everything is susceptible to taking on dramatic proportions in the polar regions. Simply running out of gas a few hundred meters from shore in a zone with a strong current can also have fatal consequences.

The Arctic is also purity. The air is incredibly clear. There are very few bacteria in polar regions, and if you want to sneeze, you have to bring your cold along with you. And the infection will soon stop, because a virus imported from a temperate country will not stand up to the cold for very long. For this reason, too, decomposition is very slow. A plant has two to three months to flower and reproduce before it is frozen again beneath the snow. Freezing is a good means of conservation, and the dead leaves of dwarfed bushes appear intact after the snow has melted the following summer.

If nature "digests" vegetable and animal detritus so slowly, the decomposition of refuse brought by humans takes several hundred years. This requires those on expeditions in

polar regions to take draconian sanitary measures. Nothing
is left on the ice, not even leftover food. Everything is sealed
up in bags, stored for the duration of the expedition, and
taken into town to be burned. As for the call of nature—
well, it is necessary to manage this so it all goes out to sea,
where scatophages will turn it anew into a source of energy.
To each his own.

Having finished our preparations, we rewarded ourselves
with a trip to the island of Blomstrand, a few miles from
Ny-Alesund. Our pretext was trying out the motors, which
had not been run for a year, and our real motivation was to
enjoy a day of rest before our trek southward in the archipelago. In the perfectly calm waters of a bay, we encountered a group of about twenty belugas. This was the first
time I had ever seen them close up, and I confess it was not
love at first sight. To be frank, their whitish backs breaking
the surface looked pretty much like big fat dumplings floating in the water.

At birth, belugas are about one and a half meters long,
and are dark brown or blue-gray in color. But as they grow,
their fur lightens to ivory. This is the reason English speakers and the Quebecois call them "white whales." The bodies
of adults can be five meters long. They have rather squarish
foreheads; almost nonexistent beaks; twenty teeth in each
of their jaws; short, curiously upward-curving pectoral
flippers; and rounded tail flukes. The only thing visible
when they swim is a little crest on their backs, in the guise
of a fin.

At first glance, belugas do not figure among the more
graceful cetaceans. The only surprise they hold in store is

an extremely mobile head, articulated on a true neck. They thus can nod their heads—they are the only small whales able to do this—but this is not enough to turn them into oceanic movie stars. They generally move slowly and peacefully, all the more so since the arctic or subarctic coastal waters they inhabit are shallow. This is particularly true of the rivers they mount for hundreds of kilometers during the summer, because they are rich in prey such as capelins, halibut, cod, and small shellfish.

While no other whale is more at home than the beluga in so little water, Tony Martin, one of the foremost experts on the subject, has shown in his painstaking work that belugas sometimes dive as deep as five hundred meters, staying down for ten to twenty minutes. Thanks to radiotelegraphy, the depth, time, and profile of the dive are recorded through a miniaturized apparatus fixed on the beluga's back. Martin realized that in the summer, pods of belugas were segregated according to their sex: females and their young in one group, adolescents apart, and adult males in a separate band. Actually, since males are larger, their lungs are more voluminous, and they can dive longer and more deeply. He thus discovered "supermarkets" a few hundred kilometers off the coast of Alaska that were off-limits to females, simply because they were unable to reach the bottom of the Arctic Ocean in these regions so rich in prey.

Typical male beluga behavior consists in descending vertically all the way to the bottom, where they spend five to ten minutes furrowing in the sand for marine worms or lying in wait for a halibut to pass by, then remounting directly to the surface to take a dozen breaths. The need to economize energy—in this case, oxygen—determines their diving behavior: distances at optimum speed, neither fast enough to run out of breath nor slow enough to lose time, and a relatively passive hunt at a depth of three hundred to five hundred meters. Then intensive oxygenation at the surface before holding their breath and returning for a good quarter of an hour's dive. By contrast, when belugas navigate along the shore, they adopt a different rhythm: one or two minutes beneath the water interspersed with single, short breaths. This is like the botos, dolphins living in the Amazon, which always remain very close to the surface. But in deep waters, the beluga adapts the rhythm of its breathing, and its behavior then resembles that of excellent divers like the sperm whale, which frequently stays under for an hour at a time after abundantly oxygenating its system with forty or fifty breaths.

The belugas' wonderful singing is certainly the most amazing thing about them. They are sometimes called "the canaries of the sea," and their vocalizations, heard underwater, sound like the whistles of a bird. I had brought a hydrophone, which permits us to hear and record sounds underwater, and thus to locate animals we cannot see. Connected to a computer equipped with the proper programs, the hydrophone furnishes information that is electronically transformed into graphics. These reveal not only the frequency of the sounds, but also the distance they have traveled from their point of origin, and their source.

The hydrophone I owned had been perfected by English colleagues who have done outstanding work in the domain of acoustics. Nevertheless, I continued to mistrust this temperamental instrument. A few months earlier, during an expedition to the North Sea, I had let my microphone down about a dozen meters below the surface in the hope of locating a pod of whales—and what did I hear but rock and roll! I had picked up a radio station in Holland. For a split second, I wondered if all the animals in the North Sea weren't also listening to the same station, frolicking about to the music of the Rolling Stones. In fact, I was not picking up the interference over the microphone; it had slipped into the electronic reception system from somewhere else. This technical problem was fairly simple to resolve, but it did not facilitate my relationship with hydrophones. Of course, for a hydrophone to be really effective, dolphins have to collaborate: for us to hear them, they have to say something. And that summer in Spitsbergen, the belugas were as silent as goldfish.

For three days, I sat in the rubber dinghy, my ears glued to the headphone, without hearing the least little warble. All the same, the group of animals contained sexually mature young adults, males and females, and I had reason to hope they would feel the urge to go courting. After all, cetacean reproduction is my specialty. But no—this bunch had no desire to contribute to my work: they kept their mouths shut. I was disappointed because I had been told so often about the beluga's vocalization and incredible whistles. So much for the recordings that could have enriched the research of colleagues still unfamiliar with the sound frequencies of belugas from Spitsbergen. In fact, every time we study the vocalization of a group of dolphins, we realize that they differ notably from those of another group of the same species. The naively astonished discourse on the so-called evolved language of dolphins is part and parcel of myth.

Delphinids show no special prowess as far as communicating by sound goes. Phony experiments close to charlatanism have taken advantage of dolphin lovers, and children in particular. For a long time, a British scientist claimed he could make bottlenose dolphins in captivity "speak." According to him, the animals were capable of using syntax—and thus of learning English. He had taught them to ask for a cup of tea. Actually, these dolphins, which like all others had no lips or vocal cords, made a kind of burping sound, followed by whistles that could vaguely resemble the series of words used to train them, provided that the listener had a lot of imagination and the willingness to believe. But it was evident that they repeated these sounds without understanding them. Moreover, what could a bottlenose dolphin possibly do with a cup of tea? All this is far from meaning that the "chatter" of dolphins, in the wild as in captivity, is not a means of communication. But to go from there to attributing to them a structured language is a matter of pure fabrication.

Nevertheless, between 1960 and 1970, several very interesting experiments took place with bottlenose dolphins in captivity. Two dolphins had been trained to recognize colored geometric shapes. When these shapes were shown to them, the dolphins activated one of two pedals immersed in their pool, according to the shape and color of the form they had been shown. The next step consisted of separating the animals by running an opaque wall the length of their pool. Only one of the dolphins could see the different shapes and colors, while the other could reach the pedals. They thus could not communicate visually, only by voice. And the game worked very well: as soon as a shape was shown to the first animal, he swam over to the wall and emitted a few whistles to his friend waiting behind it. The second animal sped straight to the pedals, activating the correct one every time. They thus relayed information by communicating with sounds.

All the same, other experiments have proven that dolphins do not possess a particularly elaborate "vocabulary" and that they communicate through supplemental means, if only through their various postures. It has furthermore been observed that many monkeys and birds use a far greater number of vocal sequences than delphinids, who do not emit more than thirty different signals per individual. On the other hand, the voice of every dolphin has a particular timbre, which allows fellow dolphins and researchers alike to recognize the individual by its whistle, without seeing it. This works like the telephone, where we recognize familiar speakers as soon as they say a single word. Moreover, animals of the same species but belonging to different population groups do not use the same sound frequencies. The "dialect" of bottlenose dolphins in Florida barely resembles the "patois" of European bottlenose dolphins.

It goes without saying that dolphins have excellent means of communication, since they are highly evolved mammals who live in groups with a complex and constantly evolving social structure. Simply said, individuals use resources other than sound signals to pass along information. For example, body pigmentation for each species, notably around the genital-anal area, varies from one individual to the next so that the animals recognize each other at a distance, even if they rarely share company. Breaching also plays a role, according to the rhythm and height of the leap and the noise the animal makes in falling back into the water. These behaviors probably serve to maintain the structure of the group and perhaps to guide it at night or in conditions of poor visibility. Breaching is probably one of the many comportments facilitating the expression of emotions. In other terms, it is certainly not necessary to be gifted with speech to make a message understood, and in this sense, animals that do not have an articulated, perfected language like that of human beings are much more sensitive to other forms of expression. The desire to make them talk only serves to maintain a myth, which in the end is less amazing than reality.

In any case, that summer on Spitsbergen I would have been at pains to establish any kind of theory about the conversation of belugas, since they were obstinately quiet. This does not mean that I lived in silence. On the contrary, after ten days on its shores, I had the impression that there was more noise on that island than anywhere else in the world. In this latitude, during the summer months, the sun never goes down, but circles the horizon with constant, unvarying brightness. And the birds take advantage of it. The common kittiwakes cry from morning . . . to morning. They never stop, they never shut up—to the contrary of my belugas. I lived in a squawking hell of gulls urgently seeking to mate, lay eggs, hatch them, and stuff their chicks' craws. They know no sleep and end up by depriving us of ours. It is imperative for them to take advantage of these two summer months, twenty-four hours a day.

Living without the pattern of light and darkness is disturbing. Little by little, you get used to a different rhythm. Why stop what you're doing at the moment, since you can continue in the same light? Why put off finishing your work until tomorrow, when no night marks the transition to the following "day"? You lose your orientation, have irregular "nights," and soon begin to dream of dawn and dusk to recover the scale of time.

When I put on my headphones to wait for a beluga's murmur, I left the racket of the gulls behind to immerse myself in an underwater cacophony. The bays of the Arctic are noisier than any other waters. Making the hydrophone vary according to different frequency levels, the "gurgling" of the fish mingles with the crash of ice as it melts, cracks, explodes, or simply gives off air bubbles. Fatigue began to overcome me, and the sounds I was hearing were so numerous and so various that I almost didn't recognize the most important one of all.

I remember sitting straight up when I heard this droll, distant complaint. I immediately recalled having heard it before, not on an expedition but in a laboratory. The sound was followed by a series of rapid "clicks." I racked my brain but still could not come up with the circumstances in which I learned to recognize these "voices." It couldn't be a baleen whale, for they do not emit clicks and are rarely found around Spitsbergen—they have all been massacred. The numerous Greenland seals and bearded seals seen on the island could not make such sounds. They were nothing like the vocalizations of belugas, either. And suddenly, a kind of groan slipped between two whistles. I jumped in my seat.

"Killer whales!"

The ornithologist who had agreed to accompany me while I was listening on the hydrophone was propped peacefully against the rubber sides of the Zodiac, reading a detective novel. He popped up like a jack-in-the-box to look around the boat.

"Calm down, I hear them—that's all. They're still a ways away."

"Are you sure they're killer whales?"

Yes, I was sure of it. A few months earlier, I had heard a recording of their cries. I'd spent several hours with a fellow researcher listening to the "discourse" of killer whales, or orcas. They were in the area, and nothing and nobody could discourage me from seeking them out. We left the bay of the phantom belugas. The wind was weak and the sea was navigable, but without our survival suits we could not safely go more than a few hundred meters out from shore. Fortunately, the hydrophone told me that the animals were staying near the coast, to port side. And in a neighboring bay, shaped like an almost perfect U, we found them. There they were: three orcas. We could immediately identify one of them, a male, by his immense dorsal fin, which was much more imposing than those of the females. On old males, they can be more than two meters high.

They had noticed us as well, thanks to the noise of our motor, but our sudden appearance in this region where they ordinarily would not encounter humans did not worry them. They didn't even seem to be surprised. The three orcas continued to explore the bay, swimming slowly along, while we stopped right in the middle of it, keeping our motor on idle all the same. I felt no real fear, but in that enclosed space, I wanted to be able to keep out of their path. Better not to provoke one of the most powerful meat eaters in the ocean.

Legends about these superpredators abound. They are capable of leaping several meters above the water—an impressive display of power. In 1950, killer whales were reputed to be so voracious that the U.S. Navy had orders to fire upon them with cannons to keep them from swallowing up entire schools of herring. Of course, orcas are incapable of decimating the fish population, and most of the apocalyptic stories about their dangerousness are false. There are no known examples of direct attacks on humans.

From a distance, we could observe them in complete safety. Their jet of vapor, which rose five meters above the surface, was clearly audible and visible, and we could clearly hear them inhaling. I had no fear that they would disappear, since killer whales rarely remain more than ten minutes underwater. The animals continued their promenade in the bay without bothering about us. Rather than hunting, they seemed to be exploring the area, as if they had just taken possession of it. At two different times, we were able to observe them very closely, first to port side, then to starboard. The big male in particular was splendid, with his inky black back and flanks, his large pectoral flippers shaped like paddles, with a white patch behind and above his eye. His tail flukes were very large, separated by a deep V. I was hoping that the females accompanying him would also be overcome with his charm and give themselves up to him before our very eyes in one of their unforgettable ballets of love. For it is the female killer whale, like the female bottlenose dolphin, who lets her suitor know when she is favorably disposed to receive his advances. She then makes a special cry, signaling the beginning of a courtship game that will go on for hours. The females take advantage of this time to savor shows of male tenderness, for after mating, the males show little interest in conjugal life. They do not become attached to the mothers or their offspring, although they defend them with great determination if danger menaces.

Orcas do not attain sexual maturity until the females are six years old and the males are seven, but like the large majority of cetaceans, they reproduce for the first time much later, when the females are ten to twelve and the males are at least fifteen. Thus it is that animals already measuring five meters long roll over, dive, and rub their flanks together in prenuptial ceremonies.

For a long time, it had been observed that females turned their white abdomens up to the surface, then disappeared beneath the imposing mass of the male, so that it was thought that they coupled only in this fashion. Later, we realized that they could also exchange positions, or else lie on their flanks.

In cetaceans, erection is voluntary, resulting from the action of a muscle. The penis of a male orca can be over a meter long. The point at which they are ready to procreate corresponds to a physical modification that is as essential as it is spectacular: in the prepubescent adolescent, a testicle weighs less than two hundred grams, while the same testicle in an adult animal weighs ten kilos.

Unfortunately, our killer whales from Spitsbergen

weren't in a licentious mood. They contented themselves
with swimming around the bay in every direction before
going out to sea again, giving our Zodiac a wide berth. The
group was very small, three animals in all, which might have
been there as scouts. There were certainly others further
out, but we did not see them. Killer whales are constantly
moving from one place to another, a factor that seems fundamental to their survival. We were not equipped to follow
them, and we did not have enough gas to go far from shore.
We went back to the beluga bay, then disembarked, for we
had promised our colleagues to lend them a helping hand
in counting their rowdy gulls.

The following morning, I would gladly have gone back
to the bay where we found the orcas, but we had arranged to
go to the Bay of Horsund in the south of the archipelago,
where we were to take the first census of colonies of nesting
birds. We had established radio contact with a Polish base
for scientific observation situated at the end of the bay.
The head of the base had invited us to pay them a visit.
Impossible to back out now—brotherly diplomacy obliged
us to go.

Our Polish colleagues had seemed joyful and enthusiastic
when we had arranged our visit, but we were met by demor-
alized men at the base, a group of prefabricated buildings
situated about a hundred meters from the shore. Just an
hour before our arrival, they had learned that the Norwegian
authorities had refused to authorize their supply ship to approach the island.

Like most of the observation posts on Spitsbergen, the
Polish base served the strategic as well as the scientific

interests of its country. Of course, the Norwegians strictly monitored foreign ships entering their territorial waters. Ordinarily, properly recorded liaison vessels receive authorization to enter, but an international agreement stipulates that no military vessel can approach the archipelago. That particular year, the Polish vessel that should have loaded at Gdansk to bring food and the relief team broke down. In an effort not to abandon the researchers on Spitsbergen, the Polish government had equipped an old corvette, which had long been disarmed. Alas, like humans, ships, too, have a legal status that follows them throughout their lives, and anyone can consult the record. This is exactly what the Norwegians did when the ship announced its intention of entering their territorial waters. The refusal was absolute. There was no question of a military vessel, even disarmed, anchoring at Spitsbergen. This would have created an intolerable precedent. And so the Polish scientists were trapped on their little corner of ice.

This was a drama for the twenty men who had been isolated for nearly a year far from their wives and children, and who shortly would run out of food. If the Norwegian government did not reverse its decision, they ran the risk of having to wait several months longer while their usual ship was repaired, in order finally to make the trip home. But in only a few weeks, the bay might well be full of ice floes, rendering any approach by ship impossible.

When we arrived, the head of the base was trying to negotiate with the governor's office. He was not pleading, but we heard the tone of distress in his voice. He first proposed that one of the corvette's lifeboats provision them with

food. This met with a new refusal: big or little, it was still
a Polish military vessel. The head of the base then had the
idea of connecting up with their own Zodiacs, as these were
already on the island. This time, the Norwegian authorities
got angry. The place of embarkation was irrelevant: if a
Polish Zodiac hooked up with the corvette, they would
consider it to be a violation of an international agreement.
The situation was blocked. Unless . . .

I don't know which one of us had the idea of propos-
ing our services, but at the time, it appeared completely
crazy. True, we owned three Zodiacs equipped with forty-
horsepower motors, but the corvette was all the same immo-
bilized twenty nautical miles from the coast: this meant
roughly fifty statute miles back and forth. That was an enormous distance to cover in little rubber dinghies, especially in
temperamental waters full of ice. And we had to make the
trip twice. But in the end, it was worth the risk.

We continued to negotiate with the Norwegians for
two more hours. They were not in favor of our interceding
because they knew that they would be held responsible if
anything happened to one of us during the operation, but
neither could they show themselves to be too intransigent.
We were French, civilians, on an official scientific mission,
and they could not consider our boats as belonging to the
Polish navy. Finally they agreed, on one condition: that only
French nationals would steer the Zodiacs. For a moment,
we hesitated, because one of our motors was coughing
enough for us not to take the risk of using it at sea. Was it
reasonable to use only two boats to transport several tons of
supplies and a dozen men? In any case, we had insisted too
much to back out, and so we gave them our word.

The operation began then and there. The Polish team loaned us waterproof survival suits, and we headed out to sea in the direction of the corvette. I am not about to forget those twenty-four hours of navigation; even if they were ultimately gratifying, they number among the most difficult hours of my life.

It all began like a remake of *Indiana Jones*. For the first twenty miles, as we headed out toward the corvette, two of us aboard each Zodiac, we let out the motors to their fullest, pleased to give ourselves over to adventure. We were playing the role of heroes and saviors. Of course it was cold, but our suits protected us well. There was some swell, but the lightly loaded Zodiacs leapt from wave to wave. And our reception on the Polish ship was worthy of a scene by Norman Mailer. Beneath a French flag expressly flown for the occasion, we drank scalding tea and vodka while the sailors loaded the Zodiacs.

Our euphoria deflated on the first voyage back. With a ton of supplies, our boats—ordinarily so lively—resembled wheezing rafts, bumping against the waves, rolling with the swell, drenching helmsman and assistant. Sprays of glacially cold water—four degrees Celsius—full of slivers of ice hit us in the face. And the cold wind transformed the mist into invisible needles that scratched our cheeks and pierced our foreheads. We were under fire from a cannon loaded with ice shards, bombarded as if riding behind a truck loaded with gravel in a heavy wind. We also had to be on constant alert for smaller blocks of floating ice detached from icebergs. Varying from the size of a paving stone to that of a small car, they had edges so sharp they could pierce the side of a rubber dinghy as easily as a razor. But with a mountain of boxes and sacks piled up in front of us, how could we see them? We were forced to navigate blind.

I think I would have given up after the first trip if the twenty members of the Polish team had not been waiting on shore. All of them were crying with emotion. And so I continued. For twenty-four hours, without stopping. Twenty-four hours is a very long time to be numb with cold, knocked about, and conscious of real danger, a factor that further increases the tension. First we got the supplies, then the men. When I got out of the skiff at the end of this epic, I collapsed in the snow. The sailors had to support me all the way to the base, where I finally could take off the suit in which I had been encased for so long. Too cold. Too tired. I could no longer control my muscles.

After a good hot shower, an hour's nap, and a thick layer of ointment on my ice-burned cheeks, I rejoined my companions and the members of the new Polish team. Only the head of the team and his assistant remained. It was my intention to get a quick bite to eat before going back to sleep, but our hosts did not agree. They intended to pay us homage in their own way. They had pinned a French flag on the wall of the room that served them as a refectory, and as soon as we entered, they began to sing "La Marseillaise." The date was July 14, 1989, the bicentennial of the French Revolution. And the Polish knew all the verses of our national anthem! Next, the head of the base called for silence, in order to give an official speech, this time in English. To listen to him, we had saved all of Poland and deserved to be treated like national heroes. Later, he gave us a medal to mark the occasion and, above all, he made us a tomato salad.

Tomatoes on Spitsbergen, where nothing grows! A dish rarer and much more precious than a scoop of caviar, when you've eaten nothing fresh for weeks on end.

This improvised ceremony was the most moving I have ever attended.

And I kept the medal.

After the Polish episode, we explored the bay. I kept hoping to see orcas again, but the animals never came back, and my hydrophone never detected their presence. I had to wait several years before I was able to get involved with them again. And when I finally did, the circumstances were rather surprising.

Where There's a Will, There's a Way

One day, I received a letter—and every year, I receive more than three hundred letters from students asking me to help them "work with whales and dolphins," plus innumerable telephone calls. Most of them request an internship or propose volunteer work. I read all the letters, of course, but my assistants answer them, and we rarely can satisfy a request. Nevertheless, this particular letter was so strange that I wanted to meet the person who wrote it. The essence of it was that my correspondent was about to finish his studies in agricultural engineering at Dijon. He needed to propose a subject for his thesis, but rather than studying the metabolism of the potato parasite, he wished to discuss killer whales instead.

As far as I could recall, Dijon was not a seaport, and I didn't see very clearly how doing research on a marine mammal could help someone who intended a career in agriculture. The author seemed to be quite an original character, and I set up a meeting with him at the Center for Research on Marine Mammals in La Rochelle. His name was Christophe Guinet.

On the stated date, not one but two characters entered

my office. One was Christophe, and the other was his professor, who had insisted on accompanying him as if to prove to me that his student was neither a joker nor a liar.

Truly, Christophe did not at all seem like a charlatan. And he resembled even less a thoughtless adventurer dying with impatience to track down orcas in every sea on the planet. He looked more like a big teenager. While he must have been past his twentieth birthday, I would have guessed he was about fifteen years old.

But as soon as he began to explain his project, I forgot all about his appearance and his studies in agriculture. The passionate determination in his voice held my full attention. He was daring, and he knew what he wanted to do. I was sure he would not want for willpower. Later, Christophe told me that he came from a family that prized imagination and creativity. His father was forever inventing things, and the family garage looked like the laboratory of a mad scientist. It ran in his family: he thought that the future belonged to dreamers. And he was right.

Meanwhile, he needed a helping hand. Without promising him anything, I decided to help him out by putting him in touch with two of my Canadian colleagues, Michael Biggs and John Ford, who had been working with orcas for fifteen years on the west coast near Vancouver. Their laboratory had already acquired an international reputation, and many students requested internships there. Maybe my colleagues, like me, would be impressed by the passionate but very lucid interest of my "protégé."

A few months later, Michael Biggs gave him a positive response. Christophe was in seventh heaven. He had shown himself to be persuasive and had also proven his efficacy in personally financing his trip and in coming up with a sponsor willing to give him a tiny inflatable dinghy with an asthmatic motor. It was better than nothing: Christophe thereby showed his motivation and, to a certain measure, he would be autonomous. And he jumped at the opportunity.

Christophe thus joined up with Michael's team, participating over the summer in the work they were doing with two schools of killer whales having different behaviors and different morphological traits. My colleagues thought one of these to be permanent residents off the shore of British Columbia, where the school concentrated during the summer in the straits full of salmon returning from migration. The other fed principally on marine mammals, and only occasionally visited the British Columbian coast.

The studies were very far along, but little observation had been done during the winter because of the severe weather. In the field, living conditions were more than a little precarious—twelve square meters of wooden cabin on a deserted island. Motivated by his passionate interest, Christophe showed his willingness, but the truth of it was that Michael didn't quite take him seriously. Since he didn't really know what to do with Christophe at the end of the summer, he told him: "If you want, you can stay at the cabin during the winter and work." He was sure the little Frenchman would go home. It takes more than nerve to transform yourself into a hermit at the far end of the Canadian wilderness. What's needed is an iron will. And it helps to be a little crazy. Christophe had both of these qualities, and he accepted without hesitation.

All winter long, he stayed alone with the killer whales, the howl of the storms, the silence of the snowfalls, and the cold. The agricultural student from Dijon took up the mantle of the solitary vagabond found in the novels of Jack London. For weeks on end, he observed the orcas, and above all he listened to them ceaselessly, shut up in his cabin with a third-hand cast-iron stove and sounds heard over the hydrophone from underwater microphones placed all along the island coast. The bay was chockfull of microphones, and he heard things that no one had ever heard before. With almost no experience or specialized scientific training, Christophe conducted the first winter study of the orca population—and the sound of fishing boats throughout the area. When he got back, he told me he was able to recognize every one of them. "I couldn't control myself," he said. "'Puff, puff, puff'—that was John's boat. 'Chug, chug, chug'—that was Jack's. 'Bam, bam, chug'—it was Alan!" But in the end, the most extraordinary thing about the adventure was that Christophe modified the conclusions of Michael's excellent team. The school of orcas thought to reside in the area in fact stayed only for a season, while the orcas the team had thought were only passing through could be observed there all year round. This was decisive work for understanding the behavior of the species.

When he understood the importance of his work at the end of the winter, Christophe hurried to Michael's to tell him the news. He descended on the home of my Canadian colleague looking like a wild man. Michael barely recognized him, with his beard, his shaggy mop of hair, and his hermit's rags. His island cabin was not only minuscule—it

was also unequipped with a shower. One time only, on a
bright sunny day, did Christophe attempt to take a bath in
a big enameled steel tub posed on stone blocks. He lit a fire
under it after filling it full of seawater. Thinking the water
was warm enough, Christophe undressed and quickly
hopped into the tub. He jumped out immediately, leaping
like a jack-in-the-box, with burns on the soles of his feet.
The surface of the water was almost cold, but the bottom
of the tub was white hot from the hearth he had lit under-
neath it. There was no second attempt at taking a bath.
So, before Christophe could explain his theory, Michael
promptly pushed him into the bathroom, where he spent
a long, restorative visit.

Even if Christophe did not profit personally from his
decisive observations of the comportment of killer whales,
his experience in Canada served him as a foundation for further studies. Ever since his wintry island sojourn, he has
been continually traveling, observing, studying, and publishing. His works have become major sources.

Ever since this time, it has become difficult to speak seriously about orcas anywhere in the world without citing
the name Guinet. Thanks to him, we now know that a
young killer whale is not entirely taught by its mother. It
stays closely associated with her for five or six years, and
she teaches it all the essentials, but it can also learn specific
skills from other females in the group, which are often more
experienced than the mother. Certain individuals specialize
in behaviors like camouflage, lying in wait for prey, or voluntary beaching, and these animals educate the young. Not
only is it true that orcas do not all behave in the same way in

every sea on the planet; in the heart of any one group, some animals distinguish themselves by being more adept than others at tracking prey, or else in locating, approaching, and driving it toward other members. Each one has its role in certain kinds of hunting, and perfect coordination has been observed among different members of the same pod, or even among several different pods when the abundance or size of the prey necessitates the collaboration of more than one matriarchal unit. The techniques they use are not fixed, but evolve over time and differ according to the group. This variety is certainly the best testimony to the intelligence of killer whales, in the sense that they are capable of learning from their experience. The study of the sounds they emit further proves this.

A researcher had recorded all the sounds made by killer whales in captivity, then reproduced them in associating each one with an object or an action. The animals quickly understood the "sense" of the sounds they could make, and they especially showed they were able to elaborate an elementary syntax, using sounds to signify, for example, "fish" and "want" when their trainer let the hour of their usual dinnertime go by. This was a very interesting experiment, because for the first time a dolphin could ask its trainer for something: the communication was not only one-way, from human to animal. The fact that orcas have an extremely efficient system of communication is not enough to allow us to conclude that they possess a real language. Their vocalizations are insufficiently sophisticated to confirm this. The vocalizations of blackbirds are ten times more elaborate than those of killer whales, and it never crosses anyone's mind to say that blackbirds are "talking" to one another or, even less, that they are trying to talk to human beings when they sing.

Killer whales' ability to memorize and share information is also revealed in the games they invent, or in the way they have of fleeing when they've a mind to do so, even though they have no dangerous predators in nature. When they want to disorient passengers on a boat approaching them, one orca or several of them appear at the surface near the boat and swim conspicuously in a given direction, while the rest of the group heads out deeper underwater in another direction. This is a true luring strategy, designed to keep anyone from understanding where the larger part of the group is located and the definitive direction it has taken. To pull it off, communication not only has to function perfectly, it also requires a leader to orchestrate the strategy.

From this point of view, the cohesion of the group is the decisive factor. Although territories sometimes extend over four hundred kilometers, in every case there is deep solidarity among the animals. In 1965, fishermen in British Columbia captured a large male killer whale and sold it to a dolphin park for eight thousand dollars. To deliver it to this establishment, they placed it in a floating cage and towed it for seven hundred kilometers. The members of his pod accompanied the captured animal for the entire length of the two-week voyage without ever flagging. Throughout this time, they continued to communicate with the "prisoner," emitting cries that the fishermen heard day and night.

In the same way, when they were hunted for their very fine oil—a four-ton orca furnishes a ton and a half of oil and two tons of meat—and a calf was killed, the mother was almost certain to be seen circling the area for days on end. Even if the mother was mortally wounded, she stayed with her calf rather than fleeing. Twenty-five years of observation in British Columbia for Michael Biggs and his team, and ten years of work on the Crozet Islands for Christophe, have shown that a pod of orcas corresponds to a veritable family whose members are most often closely related.

It is also thanks to Christophe that we now understand this species' hunting techniques, through the studies he carried out in the Indian Ocean while living in the Crozet Islands. One of these, beaching, is very particular. Christophe has acted as an adviser for superb films showing packs of orcas organizing to capture penguins or young elephant seals gathered together on the shore. The images are spectacular. Enormous predators silently lie in wait all along the shore, mounting a "siege" on the bay, with females and adolescents near the shore and large males patrolling further out. When they locate waves from a young, imprudent seal splashing about in the shallows, they head right for it with tremendous speed, leaping out of the water to seize their prey on the shore, surprising it in the exact place where it thought it was safe. The female in the group most gifted in this technique trains the calves in the water, teaching them how to beach themselves on her back before putting the lesson to the test on shore. It is there the danger lies, for if an orca beaches too well, it will not be able to get back in the water, despite all the energetic movements of its tail.

The technique has been perfected, but all individuals who try it do not arrive at the same happy results. The proof is in the skeletons found on the beaches. Awkward killer whales have beached themselves and ended up stranded. When this is the case, they die a long, painful, and horrible death. Their skin dries up and, no longer supported by the water, the animals die, suffocated by their own weight. Their agony is comparable to terrible burns in humans.

Christophe witnessed one of these failed beachings at Crozet. One morning when he was setting up his microphones in the bay, he heard strange cries. A young female had beached herself with a little too much enthusiasm and had been unable to catch the wave that should have carried her back out into the water. A few dozen meters from shore, her mother was helplessly swimming around in circles, waiting for the inevitable death of her young one. With other members of his camp, Christophe was able to pivot the orca around, so that her head was turned toward the bay. Little by little, they managed to push the animal, which already weighed over a ton. Finally, she was caught up in a wave and went back to her mother. The video of this rescue shows Christophe, soaked from head to foot, leaping for joy on the beach as the orca slides to safety.

Christophe has passed numerous seasons on the Crozet islands observing orca behavior and its evolution. Several times while a group of orcas were learning how to beach themselves on shore, young researchers went boot-high into the water in order to get closer to these superb dolphins. There they were, side by side, only a few meters away, each observing the other. It requires a lot of nerve to go face to face with a carnivore weighing several tons that does not hesitate to go after prey larger than itself. But Christophe

sensed that the killer whale was not "programmed" to attack this strange-looking thing, with two long paws sticking
in the water and a funny-looking shape above the surface.
Even a superpredator stops to consider before risking combat with an animal whose behavior and reactions are unknown to him. If we try to imagine what a killer whale
could be thinking, it must go something like this: "Is that
thing edible? What end should I start with?" But from
meeting to meeting, as fear was calmed by habit, Christophe
had the impression that the animals had begun to reflect
like this: "I can always try to bite it to see how it tastes and
reacts." At this point, Christophe and his companions immediately and definitively stopped going into the water in
front of killer whales. He had no desire to flout them, and
even less to come back legless from the mission that permitted him to put the finishing touches on his observations in
order to defend his thesis.

Did the orcas really intend to attack them? Christophe
couldn't tell, and preferred to remain in ignorance. A priori,
humans are not on their "prey list." On a first encounter, if
the killer whales do not feel endangered, there is no reason
to attack a human. But if they get a little hungry, and see
people every day in the area where they usually go to hunt,
nothing says that they won't be tempted to add this regular
visitor to their "list." Maybe, just one time, to have a little
taste . . .

The orca has acquired the stupid reputation of being the
wolf of the seas, of holding the record for voracity, because
in certain places, at certain times, it dares to attack birds or
marine mammals, and does not remain satisfied with fish,

cephalopods, and crustaceans like other whales and dolphins do. It also hunts dolphins and seals in organized packs. It kills them with a bite of its fangs, strikes them a blow with its muzzle, or projects them into the air and batters them with its tail before devouring them. The remains of eight porpoises were found in the stomach of a captured killer whale; it was impossible for it to have eaten them all at the same time, and even though we do not know the precise rhythm of a killer whale's digestion, we suppose that these were the remains of several days' worth of hunting.

Six killer whales were observed off the coast of California chasing a group of sea lions, which were frantically trying to reach the shore. The orcas would catch them and amuse themselves by tossing them out of the water with a bat of their tails. When they had had enough of playing games with the underdogs, they surrounded the sea lions and managed to kill them all before they reached the shore. From our point of view, such scenes appear to be cruel, but these game-playing activities play an essential role in learning hunting techniques. In the Arctic, narwhals, a favorite prey of killer whales, take refuge in the narrow channels between the ice floes, where their predators do not dare to penetrate. But it sometimes happens that even ice doesn't stop a killer whale. Not only do they band together to tip a big block of floating ice on which a seal has taken refuge; they are also capable of surging up from the bottom to hit an ice floe with their heads, shattering it in the place where their prey is relaxing, unconscious of danger. Even more surprising, when the block of ice is too large to be shattered with a bang of the head, the orca speeds toward it so quickly that it creates an artificial wave that breaks over the ice, sweeps its surface, and drags the resting seal into the water. From there, the orca has only to gobble up the unfortunate pinniped.

Christophe's fieldwork has debunked many received ideas—those about communication, for example. When a killer whale captures its prey, it makes a special cry, a cry of excitement, which has the power to attract the rest of the group. The prey is then shared among them. It was thought that they were calling their fellow creatures, but at Crozet, Christophe noticed that certain individuals do not cry as loudly as others, or that they remain totally silent after a successful hunt. In fact, they were stifling their cries, and from that point on, they showed themselves to be much less altruistic. They hid their joy in order to go off and devour their prey alone, without having to share it.

Christophe has opened our eyes to a species about which we knew very little. Today, orcas have become very popular, although they remain mysterious. Their technique for skinning penguins is without compare. When an orca captures one, it plays with the penguin like a cat with a mouse. Skin and feathers soon float to the surface, where giant petrels and sea gulls squabble over them. We still don't know how the orcas do it. What phenomenal skill! There is much to discover yet, and much to learn. It will take more than one Christophe Guinet to exhaust the question.

Today Christophe is a well-recognized doctor of science who excels in the domain of animal behavior and acts as adviser to other young doctoral candidates. From now on, his efforts will be aimed at studying fur seals, in the hope that elements of his work will help establish better ways to diagnose the state of our oceans, and hence of the planet. When we get together, if we happen to speak about that first meeting when Christophe came to my office chaperoned by his professor, he tells me that I allowed him to take the first step in the direction he wanted to explore. This flatters me, of course, but deep down I know that we never help those who are not already well advanced on the path they have set for themselves. He knew how to open the right door. Other students need to show the same boldness. May every one of them be moved by a truly passionate interest, the kind that makes us determined enough to persevere in spite of pitfalls. We want ten, twenty, a hundred Christophe Guinets. We truly need them.

Everything Is Yet to Be Discovered

W hy do you study cetaceans? They have all been discovered; you will never find anything new." This is
what people say to me sometimes. Of course, I could have
been an entomologist and uncovered some strange insect
every month—an obscure mosquito from Siberia, a larva
from Borneo that has never been classified, a beetle from
the Amazon that has not yet entered the nomenclature.
Perhaps I might have been happy about these things, but
I never would have been as happy as I was when one day,
before my very door, we discovered a group of all but unknown dolphins. It was as if a specialist of African wildlife,
standing at the door of her tent at a bend in a dusty road,
had discovered a pride of "new" big cats that had never
been seen in the country before.

It all began like an adventure story, just a little more
than a century ago . . .

On a beach at Sarawak, in the northwest of the isle of
Borneo, an English physicist happened to find a funny-
looking skull resembling that of a dolphin. He picked it up
and sent it to a warehouse of biological samples in London.
The British Museum bought the sample, which was quickly

forgotten on a shelf. Fifty years later, Dr. F. C. Fraser, a famous biologist at the museum, rediscovered the skull, and hesitated: this droll-looking noggin did not belong to any known species of dolphin. What was it then? Could it be a hybrid? Fraser hemmed and hawed a long while, and finally came to a decision: "The skull belongs to an unknown species of dolphin," he declared. And for this we had to wait until 1956! He described this new species, giving it the scientific name of *Lagenodelphis hosei*, but everyone called it Fraser's dolphin.

Fifteen years went by, and still nobody knew what the dolphin looked like, because they only had the description of the skull. No one had seen one alive—no one, that is, who was able to make the connection with this new skull. Suddenly, in 1971, as if by miracle, nine specimens of this new species were accidentally captured in the tropics of the Pacific and Indian Oceans. The same year, two individuals were washed ashore, one in Japan, the other in Taiwan. Six researchers immediately started studying the remains, which were more or less fresh, and in 1973 Bill Perrin and his colleagues published the first morphological description detailing its pigmentation, the anatomy of its sexual organs, and its stomach contents and parasites. Not much, but better than nothing. From this point on, Fraser's dolphin interested all cetacean specialists; scientific observations, all of them short-lived, followed one after the other. The species still remained rare. It seemed to be sighted everywhere, but it was never the right one. Fraser's dolphin was becoming an elusive tease. In 1984, nearly a century after the skull was discovered at Sarawak, everything we knew about the animal

could be summed up in a few bits of information gathered
from only twenty specimens and a couple dozen observations, all of them performed in the tropical waters of the
Pacific Ocean, the Caribbean Sea, and the Indian Ocean.

On May 29, 1984, Breton fishermen from Côtes-
d'Armor reported a group of thirty dolphins near Tégor, in
the Jaudy estuary, which opens into the English Channel.
The tide was rising as the animals entered the estuary and
tranquilly made their way up to the outskirts of Tréguier. A
tragic error. The area is dangerous—twenty-two careless
pilot whales had met their death in the region only a few
years earlier. Here, tidal currents reach five and a half kilometers an hour under maximum weather conditions, which
was the case at the end of May 1984, when the tidal range
exceeded seven meters. The tide rises quickly and subsides
just as fast, turning the Jaudy estuary into a trap. On May
30, ten dolphins from the group observed the evening before were stranded near the island of Loaven and died stuck
beneath the oyster-farming tables. Later, an eleventh cadaver
was found on the island of Poules. All of them were Fraser's
dolphins.

The smallest specimen was a five-year-old, sexually im-
mature male measuring 2.13 meters; there were six other
mature males and three mature females, the largest of which
was 2.52 meters long. At sixteen, she was also the oldest of
the group. In looks, the animal resembles the *Lagenorhynchus*
dolphin, although it is more streamlined. It has a short
beak, a mildly receding melon, and a slight concavity just
behind its head. Its flippers are small, and it is gray-colored,
a bit darker on the back than on its flanks, with a white

stomach from the chin down to the genital-anal slit. A dark line starting from the melon overhangs the eye, then runs down along its flanks to meet its tail flukes.

This was the first time Fraser's dolphins had ever been seen in moderately cold waters, and they were probably there because of exceptional weather conditions. As a result of unforeseen circumstances, it became possible for us to examine a very large group of animals from this mysterious species and to collect data on its distribution, taxonomy, reproduction, nutrition, and its parasites. The skulls from all ten specimens were collected, but only three skeletons were preserved. After the disagreeable work of cutting apart the carcasses, the bones were immersed for three days in running water in order to clean them of blood. Then the skeletons stayed in a hot-water bath at thirty-eight degrees Celsius for nearly six weeks, until they were completely clean and free of grease. They dried at room temperature for a week. The Center for Research on Marine Mammals at La Rochelle has one of the best collections of the species in the world. It is an exceptionally rare experience to find oneself face to face with a new species of a large, highly evolved mammal. On land, it is almost unimaginable. But at sea, anything is possible, and chance can still bring about surprises of considerable size.

In January 1991, *Marine Mammal Science* published an article describing a new species of Odontoceti, the pygmy beaked whale, from ten skulls gathered on the Peruvian coast. Only two animals had been discovered recently enough after their death to permit scientists to describe their external appearance. Since the adults were from three and a half to four meters long, how did it happen that such a large animal could go unnoticed until the end of the twentieth century in a region where there are so many ships? More recently yet, in 1995 another beaked whale was discovered on Robinson Crusoe Island in the Juan Fernandez archipelago off the coast of Chile. The skull clearly indicates that this species is different from those we have so far identified, but no living specimen has been observed, and we have not even discovered a dead one. How many years will we have to wait before knowing what this dolphin looks like? And how many years will go by before a new dolphin is described? The idea that it is still possible to discover new inhabitants on our planet fascinates me, even if it is an unknown mosquito in the wilds of Siberia or an orchid lost in the heart of the Amazon, and this is all the more true when it's a question of animals as fascinating as dolphins.

Maybe one morning on the Minimes beach at La Rochelle, an unknown dolphin will stick up the point of its snout in front of the windows at the Research Center. This is a dream, yes—but it certainly is not the stuff of science fiction.

It was precisely to put these surprise appearances to use—although they are sad, of course, since the animals are dead—that Raymond Duguy, director of the Oceanographic Museum of La Rochelle (closed in 1992), set up the Stranding Network to discover animals washed ashore along the Atlantic coast of France. At the beginning of the 1970s, when he realized that rare cetaceans were drifting onto our beaches, he launched a program to educate observers—gendarmes, firemen, the personnel in Maritime

Affairs, and the communal authorities—along the coast; everyone was to sound the alert in the case of strandings. This effort was meant to better our knowledge of animal life, since very few species of cetaceans other than porpoises had at that time been noted on the shores of France.

Bit by bit, during twenty years of activity, the Stranding Network has fulfilled its function and more. The Center's "correspondents," as we call them, are wonderful people. All volunteers, interested only in learning about the animals of their region, they are always ready to help us when sea mammals are stranded; some have been following our work for more than twenty years. Without them, the Center at La Rochelle could not claim to possess one of the most beautiful collections in Europe, or one of the most important data banks on the subject. The Stranding Network is a precious asset because it allows us not only to discover new species off our coast, but also to uncover problems due to overfishing, or to rapidly trace the illnesses to which whales, dolphins, and seals sometimes fall victim.

This is work of immense importance, largely surpassing a framework of study concerning only a few species. Mammals are the best biological indicators in the marine environment. If they are sick, then the fish are probably sick too, and so are the plankton and maybe even the water itself. When dolphins sneeze, the ocean catches a cold. Without our volunteer network, which has become a kind of permanent and systematic thermometer, we would be incapable of finding out if the problem we have noted is major or minor, limited or generalized. We function like the air pollution patrol in big cities: it is necessary to take samples every day, at fixed times, if we want to know whether we are threatened by danger at any one moment. And so, no matter where the call comes from, or when it comes in, be it day, night, or weekend, and no matter what state the animal is in, we always go. Except in cases of very advanced decomposition, the autopsies we perform tell us whether the specimen was ill, and if the illness could have caused its death. We take samples of teeth, which indicate age, and other samples to study genetics, pathology, reproduction, and pollution.

And sometimes we get a really big surprise. In 1996 we received a fax from a fishing boat crossing the sea off the coast of Vendée, informing us of the presence of a "big gray animal" that our correspondent could not identify. A few hours later, a telephone call signaled a "rose-colored seal" on the rocks near the first sighting. Gray, then rose. At first I thought it was two different animals, although I know from experience that most of the time when I receive two alerts in succession, they are sightings of the same specimen. But I know of only one species of marine mammal that changes color when it goes from sea to land. This is the walrus, which darkens in the water because its blood no longer irrigates its epidermis. When it stays long enough on shore, or the air warms up, its blood rises toward the outer layers of its skin. A walrus in France? Impossible. It was like imagining an orangutan strolling in the Alps, or an ostrich gamboling in the Parisian countryside, without their having escaped from the zoo. Walruses only like ice floes, frosty shingled beaches, and the big, fat clams they suck up from the mud, breaking the shells with their jaws. Their enormous, curved tusks uniquely serve as grapnels for crawling on ice or rocks, or as a display of strength. The species comprises about 207,000 animals divided between two distinct populations, one of about 200,000 in the Pacific and the other comprising about 7,000 in the Atlantic, but both are localized in arctic and subarctic regions.

The next day we got another call, this time from a correspondent from La Palmyre, near Royan. Yes, the creature on the beach was certainly a walrus, and it weighed more than a ton. When my colleagues got there, the animal was barely alive, comatose, not quite a "goner." It was horribly thin, and its skeletal structure was visible in places. The alarming diagnostic left no room for hope. We decided to euthanize the animal to put it out of its misery. I detest anesthetizing an animal knowing that it will never wake up again. The autopsy we performed on the spot permitted us to diagnose a case of generalized blood poisoning. A genetic analysis made from other samples revealed that the walrus came from Spitsbergen. It was ill, maybe even before coming south, which is probably the reason it headed out of its familiar territory. For whatever reason, it died on our shore, five thousand kilometers from the place where it was born.

We also discovered a female orca in Saint-Gilles-Croix-de-Vie, the first stranding of the species in France. She weighed four tons, and we had to transport her back to La Rochelle in a truck. We did an autopsy on her and kept her skeleton to further enrich the Center's collection. But you can't dissect an adult killer whale as if it were a frog in a laboratory. No table is strong enough to support it, and our premises were not large enough to work on an animal that took up as much space as two small cars. The autopsy and then the quartering took place in the courtyard of the Center. Some of our neighbors still remember seeing the blood run under our gate before getting a whiff of the curious smell so particular to cetaceans. To collect the major organs of such a large dolphin, our smallest scalpels are the size of a butcher's knife, and in cases when we don't want to preserve the skeleton, we take care of it with a saw. The blubber of marine mammals has a very strong odor that impregnates everything it comes in contact with, and it is very difficult to get rid of it. To "operate," we wore oilskin pants and jackets, gloves, and of course the indispensable rubber boots. At such times, our laboratory looks more like a slaughterhouse. But this, too, is part of research—at least the kind that is dedicated to more than examining slides under the lens of a microscope, the kind not satisfied with knowing dolphins and whales through the filter of technology or columns of statistics. To get the results we desire, our research needs to be grounded in the physical world, and we do not hesitate to plunge in—literally—up to the elbows.

Not all surprise strandings are as difficult to endure as that of the walrus at La Palmyre or the killer whale from Saint-Gilles-Croix-de-Vie. For a long time, we had a custom of taking in seals and housing them at the Oceanographic Museum at La Rochelle. Now, however, Cachou, the male that I saw almost daily for fifteen years at La Rochelle, and Maggie, the female, are living the life of Riley in the pools at the zoological park at Vincennes. If we are no longer taking in year-round boarders, we do continue to take in weakened, sick, and wounded animals discovered on our shores, and take care to return them to their natural

environment in better shape—in good health, well nour-
ished, and, especially, free of any dependence on human beings. But this is a lesson we learned at great cost.

Twenty years ago, we came to the rescue of a young or-
phaned seal in a pitiful state. It was a skinny little female,
too weak to eat without help, with a cold that threatened to
turn into a fatal case of pneumonia. In a few weeks, thanks
to a well-adjusted diet and daily care, she got back her
strength—and her power to charm us. A young seal is irre-
sistible. I melted at the sight of her big black eyes, and
whenever she came over to me, I allowed myself to pet her
brown fur for a few minutes. She was such a sweetie! You
should have seen her roll over and lie on her back, asking to
be tickled on her chest and belly. Seals are mammals just like
us, and so we are particularly sensitive to their expressions,
especially when it comes to charm. We were reduced from a
team of caregivers to a bunch of besotted admirers stuffing
her with fresh fish. After a few weeks of this treatment, she
was fat and fit, and we finally found the courage to return
her to the wild off the tip of Brittany. Of course, we were
proud of our work, but most of all we were sad to see her
slide into the ocean and leave us for good. Or so we
thought.

A week later, we received a telephone call that I will
never forget. Our caller began by asking us if we took care
of "lost sea animals," and we replied that we did.

"That's a good thing, because there's a seal here. I'm in
a phone booth at Le Conquet and I'd better tell you there's
a storm going on here. It's very windy, it's raining cats and
dogs, I'm the only person around, and I don't have the
faintest idea what to do with this seal."

"Where is it, on the beach?"

"No, it's with me."

"What do you mean, it's with you?"

"It's here, at my feet, in the phone booth. It was crying so loudly at the door that I let it come in with me. You're going to come, right?"

"Of course. How did you find it?"

"I was walking on the beach. I like to take walks when it's windy like this. The sea gets all white with foam, then the wind starts to whistle and . . . well, to make a long story short, the seal was there, and when it saw me it waddled right over as fast as it could come."

"The seal came over to you?"

"Oh, yes! I promise you, it wasn't my fault. It not only came to me, it won't leave me alone. It's been following me around everywhere for a quarter of an hour. You're really coming to get it?"

"We're on our way."

"Good, because this creature here won't let me budge a step."

Of course it was the young female seal we had found. We had cared for her as we should, fed her as we should. We had made only one mistake before returning her to the ocean: kindness. By allowing her to rub up against us, feeding her by hand, and taking time out to pet her, we had upset the rules of the game, and now we were paying the price of our heedlessness. If we had wanted to turn this seal into a pet, this would have been the right method. But we had always said we wanted to return her to the wild. And in that sense, we acted thoughtlessly. Our protégée had no need for affection. On the contrary, without being brutal, we should have helped her keep her instinctive fear of humans—a healthy fear. Given the circumstances, she not only saw us as care-givers but also as automatic fish distributors. The first time she encountered problems at sea in feeding herself or escap-ing a storm, she naturally came back to humans for assis-tance. Luckily, her path crossed that of a man out for a walk who was kind and well informed and knew our number. She could just as easily have come upon one of the brutes who wander along the coast with guns in their fists taking potshots at seals. Only recently, we had to treat an animal whose skin was badly scarred from shotgun lead.

So we went to pick up our protégée, and this time we behaved unpleasantly long enough so that she was fed up, mistrusted us, feared us, and wanted, on her own, to get away. You can't believe how hard it is to be disagreeable to a young seal! Nowadays, I no longer let myself be enticed, although I can't keep myself from feeling tenderness at the sight of an animal rolling from one side to the other to take in the sun. Our entire team is now under orders to observe the animals we care for from a hidden position, to throw them fish without showing themselves, not to talk to them, to ignore them or chase them away when entering their pool . . . and we return them to freedom unharmed.

We've not had any more news about our protégée, and silence is sometimes a good thing. If someone returns the tag that one of our animals wore on its flippers, it means the animal is dead. One of the seals we had found, brought back to health, and freed was found a few months later by fishermen in Iceland—in the belly of a big shark they had just caught. That young seal had all the same traveled quite a distance. Working with the team at Océanopolis at Brest and my friend Vincent Ridoux, we are currently trying to better understand the movements of the seals we band. The tag attached to a back flipper is barely visible when the animal is swimming. Each one has a unique number that allows us to identify the seals that are found stranded or captured in fishing nets. We therefore also stick a numbered plate made of colored plastic on their heads, which is none too aesthetic, but is useful for recognizing the seals at a distance. We have also begun equipping them with Argos satellite transmitters, fixed to their necks with glue. We know they will lose them the next time they moult, so the transmitters won't bother them for too long. Meanwhile, we keep track of their movements by satellite. Of the first four seals we equipped like this, one left directly for Ireland; another swam up the Channel along the Brittany coast, then crossed over at Cornwall; the third remained in the Molène archipelago. We never got any news of the fourth, whose transmitter stopped working a few hours after the seal was released.

The study of stranded animals has produced more than anecdotes. Thanks to the organs collected on our beaches over the years, we have radically modified our programs for the protection of dolphins. Once again, the adventure began like a book—this time, a detective novel.

One autumn morning in 1980, I buckled my suitcase and left La Rochelle. After a stop-off in Paris, I took the train to Calais, where I embarked for England. The importance of the studies that were taking me abroad obsessed me and at the same time allowed me to put off worrying about a certain detail. But going through English customs, when I laid my suitcase on the counter, my fears awoke with a shiver. What if they asked me to open my bags? Holding my breath, I held out my passport. The officer looked at it with a practiced eye and motioned me through. I took several steps before letting out my breath. I wonder what I would have done if he had inspected my bags and discovered that half the contents were test tubes full of formalin with bits of organs floating in them. Of course, he would have questioned me: "What are you carrying here?" And, paling, I would have responded: "A few dozen ovaries and dolphin testicles, sir."

Today, it is necessary to have previous authorization to transport such material, since it concerns parts of animals strictly protected under innumerable conventions. As a matter of fact, according to the law, every time I take a tooth from a beached animal, I should request permission from the Ministry of the Environment, which applies to the Museum Council for advice, which then responds back to the Ministry . . . two to three months later. But at the end of the 1970s, there was still no ruling prohibiting samples of the sort from crossing borders. I still doubt that the customs official would have let me continue my trip without a long process of verification if he had seen the contents of my suitcase. In any case, I would have moved heaven and earth to get my test tubes back if they had been confiscated: losing them would have been like giving up my right arm. My doctorate depended on those gonads. They were to undergo appropriate testing at Cambridge, and if the results of the study confirmed my hypothesis, I would be ready to write up my doctoral thesis. For me, they were more than sexual organs floating in formalin—they were the results of two long years of work.

I had arrived in La Rochelle in October 1978. Dr. Raymond Duguy, conservator at the Museum of Natural History, had agreed to act as my research adviser during my year of study for the DEA (Diplôme d'Etudes Approfondies). The truth of it is, I had twisted his arm, since he thought he was not cut out for the role. But who, I wondered, apart from him—the only person in France who had real experience in the field—would have had the knowledge to help me write a thesis on the biology of the North Atlantic common dolphin? So I stuck my foot in his door and finally found the right words to convince him to take me on.

Raymond Duguy had set up the Stranding Network in 1972 and managed to collect samples on about a hundred dolphins every year. After I arrived, the number rose to 250 specimens, because I was already convinced that this incessant activity constituted a source of invaluable information from which we could draw decisive lessons for our understanding of cetacean behavior, and maybe more. Today, on average, in years when nothing special occurs, we annually study more than 350 specimens.

The precious loot I was taking to England was gleaned from two years of autopsies. At Cambridge University, Professor Richard Harrison, director of the department of zoology and a great scientist, had agreed to see me in his laboratory. This man, with his impressive frame and white hair, whose research and extraordinary publications were respected throughout the world, received me with great kindness and simplicity. With him, hospitality was a law no less important than the science whose rules he had so thoroughly mastered. It was imperative for me to work closely with him if my samples were to have any value: I needed to absorb the basics of histology, that is to say, the observation of cells, and especially learn how to interpret the results correctly—something that, in this domain, only Professor Harrison could teach me. To begin the study of dolphin reproduction, it is first necessary to know the age of the animals under study. Their teeth reveal this information. These are cut in thin slices along the length of the tooth, so the striation can be examined under the microscope. In general, each layer corresponds to a year of growth. I learned the techniques for reading the teeth of my specimens from Dr. Christina Lockyer, of the Sea Mammal Research Unit attached to the British Antarctic Survey, a European laboratory of world renown. Christina was one of the first to master this aspect of the work, and she shared her knowledge willingly.

With the same kindness, Professor Harrison gave me two assistants to help me in my work. And for a month, every day at noon, as he drank his pint of beer in the guise of lunch, he advised me, directed me, explained things to me. For, although I could learn the technique from his colleagues, his help was indispensable in helping me to analyze the results and interpret them correctly. Later, he even taught me to write up scientific documents that require a special methodology. Actually, my work fascinated him, as did everything having to do with dolphins. And my test tubes

really were the treasure I imagined them to be, for even
Professor Harrison himself did not have research material
of such high quality at his disposal. At Cambridge, I could
finally begin to understand how dolphins reproduced and
to support my hypotheses with irrefutable proof.

When I crossed the border coming back home, my
treasure trove of testicles, ovaries, and teeth had been transformed into a case of glass slides. I was less nervous facing
the customs officer. The extra room in my suitcase, now
empty of test tubes, was filled by an authentic English
wicker basket destined for the handlebars of my bicycle.
This was a souvenir of my weeks at Cambridge, where, like
every other self-respecting student, I dashed about the city
on an English bicycle equipped with a basket. I still use it
today.

I published my thesis in France, and as soon as I was
awarded my doctorate I returned to Cambridge at Professor
Harrison's invitation. We were to publish our research. What
pride I felt to see my name on my first scientific article, next
to that of an eminent researcher. He absolutely insisted
that I attend one of the famous dinners at the college. It
was out of the question for me to wear a dress; a doctor of
science had to wear a college gown, a convention that does
not exist in France. They loaned me a gown that was three
times too large—I tripped on the hem when I walked. As
for the meal itself, this was a ceremony I am not about to
forget. I thought I had gone back in time to find myself at
the court of Henry VIII. The refectory was a huge chapel
where two hundred uniformed students, sitting along rows
of immense tables, waited for the professors to appear. We

made our entry, walking single file according to hierarchy, and took our places on the platform facing the students. Once we were seated and I realized that the person nearest me was two meters away, I felt as if I had changed centuries again: this time, I felt as if I were at the Last Supper, but with a prayer in Latin spoken with an English accent.

Two hours of dinner, with eight or ten courses, and three wines . . . I thought it would never end, and I especially feared that the evening would be just as stiff. But not at all! Tradition had been accorded its due, and now it was time to party. The professors got out of their gowns, the students out of their uniforms. Everyone made for the bar, installed in a superb vaulted cellar, to drink beer and thump each other on the back while listening to the Beatles. I couldn't get over the fact that it was possible to create such a gulf between the "knowers" and the "learners," then dispense with it in an instant. In these ancient cellars, novices rub shoulders with the most important specialists in their favorite subjects and can approach them without risk of being rebuffed. They form a real community. To all appearances restricted by ancient rites, English professors are actually much closer to their students than the mandarins of knowledge in France.

My work in England, preceded by years of taking organ samples and followed by several months of analysis, interpretation, and writing, reached its conclusion in December 1981, in San Diego, California, at a conference on cetacean reproduction organized by the International Whaling Commission. Two hundred people were attending. Among them were the most important specialists in the area, notably Dr. Bill Perrin, the organizer of the conference. I was very impressed by him, for I had read his numerous articles, and I imagined him as an aloof big shot. In reality, he still looked like a student, with a big, ill-tended beard, and he searched me out for a discussion as if I were his equal. I couldn't believe it, and let him know my surprise. He burst out laughing and explained that he already considered himself to be an "old man"—he was barely over forty—and to avoid becoming ossified in what he already knew, he thought it was very important to talk to young people like me, principles and prejudices aside, about ideas that might sound a little crazy, but were certainly more productive and creative than those of an old man like him. Sam Ridgway and Ken Norris, recognized as experts on modern cetology, were also there. Again, I was completely taken aback when I was introduced to Dr. Ridgway, who was not the stiff personage in a suit and dark tie I had imagined him to be, but a stocky, regular guy with graying hair, wearing jeans and a cowboy hat like any other good Texan.

As for me—I was also a star! My name was on the program. I was simultaneously proud and frightened to death at the idea of going up to the podium and throwing my thesis into the lions' den of this distinguished crowd of experts. My conclusions overturned the accepted theories of the day. All the literature published on the subject of dolphin reproduction agreed that these animals were sexually mature at two or three years old. They were supposed to mate and reproduce as soon as their gonads produced gametes and they were thus physiologically capable of producing offspring. In other words, it was thought that a female two to three years old could be impregnated, and then give birth every year. Since dolphins live on average thirty years, it was thought that a female could give birth more than twenty times during the course of her lifetime. After having examined many ovaries and the scars from ovulating that mark them, I was convinced that we were on the wrong track. Before I teamed up with him, Professor Harrison also thought that the theory was false, but he hadn't been able to prove it. The organ and teeth samples I had gathered permitted us to do so. But he had not been able to come to San Diego to support me. I was alone, face to face with my peers.

And so I went up to the podium, trembling, but with proof in hand, to explain that although dolphins could produce gametes at an early age, the females did not really reach the age of reproduction until they were eight to ten years old, and the males between ten and fifteen. My research showed that dolphins did not calve every year, but once every three or four years, at most, and that it was thus an illusion to think that a female could have twenty-five offspring: during the course of her life she would have four or five healthy calves at most, given that she would go though menopause, like humans and a few other highly evolved mammals.

In spite of their relatively precocious sexual maturity, dolphins reproduce for the first time fairly late in life, because they first must reach a certain level of social maturity within a highly hierarchical group. The young engage in sexual games, quite often as a matter of fact, but there is no impregnation. The consequences of setting the record straight on this point were very important, because it meant that dolphin populations did not grow rapidly, as we imagined; on the contrary, their growth was particularly slow.

This demonstration had enormous repercussions, especially from the point of view of protecting the species. If we agree that a population of one hundred dolphins includes fifty females capable of giving birth to one calf a year, we thereby conclude that even if fifteen individuals are accidentally killed each year, the group will not be endangered. But if we know that in the best of cases, only thirty females are able to reproduce, and that they will give birth, on average, to barely a dozen young each year, then if fifteen members of the group are regularly killed every year during the same period, this same population of one hundred dolphins will very rapidly disappear.

After having tossed off my thesis as if I were unburdening myself of a load too heavy to carry, I rapidly ran through a series of mediocre slides, went back to my seat, and waited for the worst. I was expecting hisses and jeers—and, why not, a splattering of rotten tomatoes. In fact, there was only applause, but I was so withdrawn into myself, my fists clenched, my stomach in knots, that I couldn't even hear it. After all, who was I to contradict the big shots? Before this, I'd never done anything important. I sat in the lecture hall, my shoulders hunched up around my neck, grimacing a grin. It took a few minutes before I was even able to hear the following paper . . . and to understand that the young woman who had followed me to the podium was explaining that she had arrived at similar conclusions, but through a different method. I wasn't the only one! She was confirming my interpretation.

In the end, my reception at the conference was positive and straightforward. It was necessary to begin all over again in the study of dolphin reproduction—that was all there was to it.

That day, I delivered a decisive paper, but I also learned that as far as scientific research goes, there is no such thing as a "scoop." Everyone works at about the same rhythm, and every day everyone makes a little progress. Everyone gets results—some sooner, some later. Today, Michel Milinkovich, an intern at the Center a few years ago who is fascinated by genetics, thinks that the larger sperm whales, which have teeth and have always been classified as closely related to tooth whales, may be closer to baleen whales. He and his team have proven the existence of a group of "sperm-baleen whales" that had a common ancestor at the point the tooth whale family had already branched off in another line. This is a fundamental challenge to the theory of cetacean evolution. Of course, his hypothesis needs to be confirmed. And if it is proven one day, the press will probably make the results sound like a scoop. But in the scientific world, such will not be the case.

Sometimes people say to me: "Research is such slow, complicated, fastidious work. Sometimes the results are disappointing. You don't have enough funding. And fieldwork is no better. It takes you far away, it can be dangerous, you're never sure what the results of a mission will be. And there's been little progress in protecting species—there's pollution, overfishing; mind-sets don't change quickly enough, the pressures of the market slow everything down. What do you do to keep from giving up? Where are you going to find the strength to continue?"

I hear these remarks and questions often, expressed in different ways. And yes, sometimes I do lose courage—but never for long. Confidence bounces back quickly. All it takes is a few memories, a few images—memories and images full of hope. They are luminous in my mind. And I know that it's not over, that tomorrow holds other experiences that will become, in turn, more images and memories, but only if I don't give up, solely if I obstinately persist in chasing down new stories, and those occasional glimpses of fate. There are days, hours, sometimes seconds, when my heart beats hard because of some small thing—rare true moments that completely overwhelm me. Moments for tears, rage, and fury, and moments for laughter and satisfaction. My motor is the life I observe all around me and in which I participate, fueled by curiosity, surprise, admiration, and wonder.

And I say to myself that I'm really lucky to have chosen this kind of work.

Creatures of the Sanctuary

He's three meters long but weighs over a ton. He splashes about the shore but doesn't dare to set a flipper on the beach. From time to time, he's bold enough to lift up his trunk and bellow, but that's as far as it goes. A young male ten years old, he's on the lookout for any female who might be of a mind to come for a little dip. In that case, he will try to seduce her, but quickly and brutally, for the master of the domain is as vigilant as the devil. That's him over there—the boss, the macho lolling on the beach, who must tip the scales at triple the youngster's weight and measure nearly five meters long. He's not about to share his harem—there's no question about that. For three years now, the upstart has been trying to satisfy his libido in vain. If he fails this year to appropriate a female, secretly, in the water, without the bull realizing it, he will have to wait a long time again. A very long time—it will be twelve or fifteen years before he, in turn, will become a macho able to challenge the master of a harem.

This is the hard law of the elephant seal: before he is twenty-five, there is practically no chance for a male to prove his virility. No sooner will he achieve this privilege than it will be contested. And he will defend it savagely. After waiting a quarter of a century for the right to mate, he's not about to let another steal his place at sunup.

I first set foot on a subantarctic island in 1990, at the beginning of the Southern summer. The biggest males had just arrived on the beaches and were fighting on every corner of the island to claim the best territories. The battles were furious: not for nothing are male elephant seals called "bulls." They hurl themselves against each other, trunks held high and swollen with air, teeth bared. They bite, groan, lacerate, and pierce each other, groan and gash again, then flee, or triumph with a resounding belch. Overheated, they next flop down in a heap, scratch up the ground beneath them, and take a sand bath. The losers go elsewhere to challenge other, perhaps less healthy, beasts. Space is expensive, but a little later, when the ladies arrive, the lots will all be accounted for. No matter how fat they are, even if they are ready to give birth the day after their arrival, female elephant seals look almost like dwarfs next to the males. The sexual dimorphism in this, the largest of the seals, is impressive: a female weighs barely more than 550 kilos, while a male can weigh up to four tons. When it comes time to couple, their "embrace" resembles the passage of a steamroller.

Several days after giving birth to a completely black calf, the mothers are ready to receive the homage of the males again. The bulls delightedly inhale the perfume of females in heat, fight some more with their scar-covered rivals, reopening ugly, poorly closed wounds, then lurch toward their chosen ones, exhibiting their long, rose-colored penises, which at other times are pulled in so as not to slow them down in the water. For we must not forget that these awkward-looking, lumpy, furless masses of blubber are formidable hunters in the ocean, able to descend to a depth of a thousand meters to capture the fish and squid that constitute their diet. But it is true that they are not the most graceful, aesthetically pleasing animals to be seen on land. And the bull is not exactly tender. Because the female seems none too eager to be crushed beneath the weight of her hefty suitor, he has to corner her, plant his teeth in her neck to immobilize her, and make six or seven tries before he gets what he wants. It sometimes happens that the young, caught in the fray, flattened between their parents and the pebbled shore, smother without being noticed.

I wouldn't have dared to venture among the elephant seals as I had done the preceding year among a colony of fur seals on the shores of Argentina. Fur seals, too, are quick and sometimes very aggressive, but one of the young females in the group had been garroted. She probably had tried to pilfer some fish from a net, and although she had managed to tear the mesh and extricate herself from the trap, a piece of nylon remained knotted around her neck. If we hadn't intervened to capture her and cut the cord, she would gradually have been strangled as she grew. She would have died, starving and asphyxiated.

But her rescue was easier to imagine than to carry out. From the very start, her capture took on epic proportions. We had to keep her from getting to the water. If she had managed to dive, we would have lost her. But this little game did not amuse her: panicked, she bellowed, bared her teeth at whoever blocked her path, and slipped from our hands like a bar of soap every time one of us was on the verge of trapping her. There were half a dozen of us guarding her in a circle and chasing her. While we were twisting our ankles on the stones, the seal slipped over them, full speed ahead on her belly. Finally, someone threw the top of a tent over her, and we took advantage of her momentary surprise to hold her down, cut the nylon, and jump back before she managed to bite. It's better to avoid a seal's jaw—it is as powerful as a Doberman's. The chase lasted over three hours, but she was free. If one of the female elephant seals had fallen prey to a similar misadventure, we unfortunately could not have done anything for her. We would have had to abandon her to her fate surrounded by males in rut.

I had not gone south to see these Dantean ceremonies, but the spectacle of these creatures copulating left me speechless every time I witnessed it. I was careful to keep upwind of the elephant seals, which massed together in the same place for weeks on end, for the effluvia floating on the breeze would turn the stomach of a goat. With the exception of their young, which are adorable like those of all seals, a colony of elephant seals is the worst company it is possible to imagine: from dawn to dusk it is belches, defecation, shedding, snot, and farts. We quickly began to prefer observing them through binoculars from a distance.

Watching libidinous bulls was not the reason for the trips I took to Antarctica at the beginning of the 1990s. I was motivated by a dream I share with many sailors—those of us who, when winter comes and the storms blow up in the Bay of Biscay, wait out the time before we can go back on shipboard by reading tales of the sea. I had devoured the stories of Vitos Dumas, Joshua Slocum, and Bernard Moitessier, read the *Damien* trilogy by around-the-world sailor Gerard Janichon, and plunged into the world of Patrick Van God's *Trismus*, written before he was lost at sea. I wanted to see the Southern waves, the coast of the "white continent." I wanted to see the Strait of Le Maire, Staten Island, the channels of Patagonia, and Cape Horn. I wanted to see beyond Cape Horn, to Drake Passage and the peninsula. I wanted to see the animal life—bountiful, free, and still intact. I hoped to come across rorquals, particularly their most celebrated member, the longest, largest, heaviest, most fabulous animal our planet has ever borne—and also the most powerful and peaceful. I had made a date to meet *Balaenoptera musculus,* the blue whale.

I was part of a team of scientists, each with a different specialty, who had been invited to take part in expeditions during the Southern summer on a small ocean liner chartered by groups of knowledgeable amateur naturalists. They were, in fact, pioneers heading for destinations tourists can visit today. As for us, the researchers, we could carry out all the observations we wished as long as we accorded a bit of our time to our fellow voyagers. We held seminars on shipboard and accompanied them whenever they set foot in these ultra-protected areas. Fortunately, our ship had nothing to do with modern cruise liners, but more closely resembled a floating Orient-Express, fitted out with an abundance of precious wood and brass. There was no television in the cabins. It would have been impossible to dream of a better way to approach one of the most beautiful places on earth, and one of the wildest. And, in my opinion, the most exhilarating.

We glimpsed our first whale in Drake Passage. We had

left Ushuaia the evening before and rounded Cape Horn six hours earlier. It was a rorqual, but the heavy swell of the waves made it impossible for me to determine the species with any precision. One thing I do know—that whale was sleeping like a baby, taking a siesta in one of the most murderous seas in the world! I still wonder how it did it, but in any case, the sleeping habits of large cetaceans remain a mystery. We are certain of only one thing: a rorqual's brain cannot go completely "to sleep," because its breathing is voluntary. If rorquals abandoned themselves in the arms of Morpheus, they would die of asphyxiation because they would forget to breathe. And yet they sleep deeply.

The whale did not budge as our ship approached, and we could have pushed it with our bow if our captain had not preferred to keep a respectable distance to ensure that we wouldn't hurt the whale. There are numerous accounts of sleeping whales being rammed by enormous cargo ships— ships they would have heard, and of course avoided, if they had been awake. Such accidents are fatal to whales. But when the ship is lighter, most notably a sailing ship, the vessel is the one to suffer from the collision. The hull tears open and the ship sinks rapidly after the shock. This is probably the way that Patrick Van God perished at sea. Whalers frequently noted the results of such brutal encounters with ships, discovering set fractures in the ribs or vertebrae of the animals they captured and butchered.

Smaller species, dolphins in particular, do not suffer this kind of misadventure. The stories of dolphins wounded or killed by propellers are just that—stories. I have performed thousands of autopsies on animals washed up along the coast of France bearing signs of cuts, and in one case only could I attribute the cause of death to such an accident. On the other hand, the cadavers are often driven against the rocks, shredding their skin. Dolphins are agile enough, and sufficiently aware of their environment to avoid the propeller of a boat, even when they are sleeping. This is all the truer in that they travel in groups, and one member would be bound to see or hear the approach of a motor.

Nevertheless, tooth whales do not sleep as deeply as baleen whales. Electroencephalograms of bottlenose dolphins in captivity monitored over several consecutive days have shown that their periods of total repose correspond to what we would call "light sleep." Dolphins know neither deep sleep nor the rapid eye movement that signals the onset of dreams. During this light sleep, they maintain their muscular tone, which permits them to continue to engage in voluntary, albeit limited, activity, like mounting to the surface to breathe, for example. At these times, the animals' eyelids are closed. They appear to be immobile, but if you observe them attentively, you can distinguish small tail movements. These keep them just a few meters below the surface, and they come up from time to time to breathe. The rhythms of their hearts and respiratory systems slow down at these times, but their brains remain on alert. It may be that only one hemisphere of the brain remains on watch, while the other "dozes." Much study remains to be done before we can be certain.

All these facts pertain only to dolphins, for we are far from able to keep a blue whale in captivity successfully—and so much the better! The largest specimen ever captured

was almost thiry-four meters and weighed more than 150
tons. He would barely have fit in an Olympic-sized swimming pool, and even then it wouldn't have been deep enough.
Their size allowed them to escape the whaling ships until a
Norwegian, Svend Foyn, invented the harpoon cannon in
1867. After that, blue whales became whale hunters' prey
of preference. The largest specimens brought in thirty tons
of oil apiece. Up to thirty thousand a year were killed
between the two world wars, and we do not know if the
species will ever recover from the massacre. Reestablishing
the stocks is such a complicated matter that we still have
reason to fear that an ecological accident could cause them
to become extinct.

The antarctic peninsula is a strip of land one thousand
kilometers long whose tip points toward South America.
A cold clockwise current circles the continent, encounters
the peninsula, then circles it again counterclockwise, making a loop. The waters in this zone, abundantly rich, are host
to numerous species: orcas swimming among the icebergs
hunting for seals and penguins; several other species of dolphins; and sperm whales, right whales, humpback whales,
fin whales. And there are blue whales, of course, which do
not enter the bays but prefer to remain in the open sea. I was
counting on my luck to encounter these colossi, which migrate like all other baleen whales. I could reasonably hope
to cross the path of females accompanied by their young as
they returned to the icy waters rich in food. But first, we
wanted to do something—swim!

A hundred kilometers from the tip of the peninsula,
Deception Island, the southernmost of the Southern

Shetlands, looks like a crescent on a navigator's map. It is
actually an extinct volcano. An impressive narrow pass, only
fifty meters wide, forms the entrance to the bay, a kind of
inner sea surrounded by black mountains covered with
glaciers peppered with coal dust. The bay forms a natural
lock, and wild, rushing winds that sometimes seem to fall
straight down the mountainsides inspired whalers to name
it Neptune's Bellows. Entering this narrow funnel with a
ship eighty meters long gave me the shivers. It is nonetheless
the only place in the Antarctic where it is possible to dive —
or at least take a little dip.

Water with a temperature of eighty degrees Celsius
surges along the beach, heating a strip of ocean about a
meter and a half wide. You must undress very, very quickly
and rush to the right spot. Beyond the area of warmth, the
water is only four degrees Celsius. It is easy to burn your
shoulder blades and freeze your toes. But Deception Island
also had other surprises in store. The first was a visit by a
leopard seal, a strange animal that looks like a cross between
a seal and a snake. It has cold eyes, an immense mouth bristling with pointed teeth, and impressive fangs that give it a
reptilian smile. It uses these strong teeth to capture penguins underwater, then skins them by striking them against
the ice before swallowing them. Along with the killer whale,
it is the most dangerous predator of seals. The one that paid
us a visit was very peaceful, barely curious, and had obviously eaten its fill. After observing us for a few minutes, it
dived into Whaler's Bay and disappeared.

A bit later, I was the one to pay a visit. A female fur seal
weighing thirty-five kilos was lolling on the beach. In order

not to scare her away, I couldn't appear to be larger than she was, so I lay down on my stomach and crawled toward her, taking infinite precautions. At first she seemed to consent to my presence. She stayed where she was, scratching behind her ear with her long back flipper. From time to time, she turned her head to look at me and groan, but showed no hostility. After crawling toward her for twenty minutes or so, I was about ten meters away—the inner boundary of her circle of safety. Nothing obvious defined it, of course. I knew that when I crossed the line, she would change her attitude, and that this would be my only means of discovering I had crossed the invisible barrier of safety. And suddenly, with a final warning belch that put me on my guard, the seal charged.

They may look heavy and awkward in their coats of fat, with their enormous bellies and long flippers, but when a fur seal charges, it can rival a man running at full speed. I had just enough time to get up, spin around, and take off as fast as I could, praying not to stumble. A seal bite not only is painful, it can also be serious, because it tends to become easily infected. Fortunately, I did not trip on the slippery pebbles, and the seal followed me a dozen meters or so before turning around to take up her gracious pose again, looking for all the world like a sack of potatoes plopped on the sand.

The third surprise I had on Deception Island frightened me more than the charge of the irascible seal. For half an hour, I thought I had lost one of the passengers we were accompanying. She was an American, a rather pretty woman whose behavior was truly bizarre. She was very tall and slender, with long, blond hair, which she wore pulled back severely like a girl at her first communion ceremony. She could have been elegant if she hadn't dressed as if she were eleven years old. She wore full skirts and round-collared blouses. We had to threaten her to make her change from her Mary Janes into fur-lined boots before getting into the Zodiac. But all of this ultimately would have been likably eccentric if only she hadn't expressed a disturbing idea: "I have just one dream," she would repeat to anyone willing to hear. "I want to lose myself in Antarctica."

Needless to say, I kept a watchful eye on her, especially since she wore a big backpack each time we took an excursion. I imagined she had it crammed with an eiderdown, food, and maybe some books. Fortunately, all our companions were equipped with red thermal parkas, and we had no trouble locating them in the snow. I only had to count my flock from time to time to be sure they were all there. Normally, there were seven of them, and I counted them every half hour.

That day, after the charge of the fur seal, I inspected the troops and realized that someone was missing. My American had disappeared. I felt a knot in the pit of my stomach. Antarctica is certainly a protected sanctuary, but it is also a land full of every kind of danger for anyone who goes astray. It is almost unthinkable that even a man in good health could survive for more than a few hours without the proper equipment. I rushed off to look for my American and was happy to find her a few moments later, seated behind an old whaler's cabin at Port Foster. She was only lost in thought and hadn't heard me calling her name. While I told her yet again she should not go off on her own without letting me know, I realized that her big backpack, lying next to her, was open. Taking advantage of a moment when she stooped down to pick up her camera, I glanced into this sack whose contents had so intrigued me for days on end. No food, no eiderdown, no books, nothing but an enormous teddy bear! Later, one of the chambermaids on the ship told me that our American passenger owned a dozen large stuffed animals. There were bears, lions, panthers, penguins—and she probably took each of them for a walk in turn.

Every time I remember her, I think that maybe she wasn't kidding about wanting to get lost. Throughout our trip, she never gave us the slip. I watched her so closely that it would have been impossible for her to do so. But I imagine her taking the same liner the following year, without revealing her intentions. Perhaps one morning she got off at Deception Island, or King George's Island, or Petermann Island. Perhaps she fulfilled her dream.

It was while we were leaving Deception Island, two days later, that the blue whales honored us by crossing our path. Another vessel, an Argentinean military ship, had located them twenty kilometers off the island and radioed their location. We headed off in their direction and caught sight of them just before noon. We couldn't have missed them. There were three, one of them a calf. The largest must have measured a little over thirty meters. The pod had apparently just crossed Drake Passage diagonally and was taking a southwest route toward the Pacific.

We put a rubber dinghy into the water and four of us went out to meet them. I had no precise mission to accomplish at the time, and I know I approached these animals with a fast-beating heart, as if it were the first time I had ever had contact with a whale. This was probably because blue whales, every bit as much as dolphins, had always made me dream. All I wanted was to see them, to hear them breathe, as if I needed proof they had survived.

These three rorquals were utterly superb, full of serenity and power. As they calmly swam along, their backs seemed to stretch forever, their dappled gray-blue skin glistening in the sunlight. This is the color that gives them their name. A small dorsal fin about thirty centimeters long distinguishes the last third of their backs, and its triangular form helps us to identify the species. Their flippers are relatively short, and they show their tail flukes only when they're diving vertically. But when they do dive, they reveal a tail span seven meters wide.

If whales were created to trouble the human mind, then the blue whale was made to instill in us a sense of humility. All we have to do is see it blow, watch as that enormous vertical spray of vapor rises straight up in the air more than ten meters. It is the incarnation of the biblical Leviathan that "maketh the deep to boil like a pot," that swallowed, then regurgitated, Jonah. It is a living legend. When it surfaces, even those who love it and feel close to it must call upon their reason to accept the fact that the animal before their eyes evolved from a small mammal that looked like a wolf and haunted the swamps of the earth 50 million years ago. It kept its lungs, and its respiratory system adapted itself around them: all the bones of its head, as long as a banquet table, were transformed so that its nasal passage could cross the top of its skull from one side to the other. Its larynx became modified, so its respiratory and digestive systems were no longer connected. Although it can no longer breathe through its mouth, at least it can't choke.

This colossus is still warm-blooded, even though its favorite dish is served in glacial waters—a handicap for which it compensates with physiological "tricks." First, there is its gigantic size: by growing so enormous, the whale has found the ideal compromise for surviving near the poles. The gigantism of polar cetaceans is a complex metabolic solution that in fact slows down the loss of heat. Like other mammals, whales are homoeothermic and must maintain a constant body temperature in a very cold environment; water temperature in the Antarctic can go down to -1.7 degrees Celsius. They have thus also developed a coat of blubber, which can be as much as fifty centimeters thick. The parts of their bodies not protected by blubber—their tail flukes, for example—have developed a way to transmit heat through crosscurrents. The veins surround the arteries so that the blood going back to the heart recovers the heat from the blood flowing from it. This is a thermal superregulator. When all is said and done, the whale is definitely a physiological aberration—and yet it is perfect. It is an animal full of paradoxes.

One of its most amazing characteristics is its enormous mouth, six meters wide and garnished with whalebone. These horny plates attached to its palate allow it to filter the ocean, keeping in food and spitting out water. But rorquals are distinguished from other baleen whales by a series of longitudinal grooves on their throats. The blue whale has forty or so of these grooves, which run from its chin all the

way down to just behind the axis of its flippers. These act
like the bellows of an accordion to increase the volume of
its mouth. When it feeds, the throat grooves form a gigantic
goiter that looks like the pocket of a pelican's beak. It thus
filters tons of water with every gulp. The ancients thought
it ate nothing but "darkness and the rain that falls on the
sea." But, obviously, it does eat. In the Antarctic, it almost
uniquely lives on krill, shrimp three to eight centimeters
long. The Southern baleen whale population swallows
about 44 million tons of them every year. But we still don't
know precisely how much krill is necessary for their survival, or the amount of energy that represents, just as we
still have not discovered the majority of their techniques
for locating food. How do they find banks of krill? By the
sounds they make? Their smell? Do they use a radar system
similar to that of dolphins? Baleen whales devour huge
quantities of food, but they do so discreetly.

Because the blue whale's spout is seen in all the seven
seas, it is said to be a roaming monster. The truth of it is
that blue whales, like all baleen whales, could do without
the incredible distances they cover every year. Throughout
the summer, they feed in highly fertile frigid waters. Then,
as winter approaches, the pregnant females gradually stop
eating and begin their migration to the tropics. Since the
seasons are reversed in the two hemispheres, Northern
whales never encounter their Southern sisters. Summer for
one is winter for the other. It is sometimes said that the
loud vocalizations of the arctic blue whales are directed at
those in the Antarctic, but this is the stuff of fairy tales.

In the course of migrating to the zones where they give

birth, pregnant females travel as much as ten thousand kilometers, barely eating a thing. They swim at about sixteen kilometers an hour, but they can reach a speed of thirty-two kilometers an hour if they feel threatened. Blue whales do not get too near the coast, and their zones of reproduction are not as well defined as those of other whales. Once a female has arrived in the warmer waters of the Atlantic or the Pacific, she gives birth to a single calf after twelve months of gestation. In the course of her life, a female will give birth to a maximum of five viable calves. The calf is birthed tail first, for if it came head first, it would have to hold its breath until it was completely delivered, and so would risk dying. Then its mother helps it reach the surface, where it breathes for the first time.

The female nurses her young for seven to eight months, the first week with a daily dose of five hundred liters of milk, which consists of 50 percent fat, or butter. Cetaceans do not have lips to nurse their mothers like other mammals do. The problem is resolved by a muscle surrounding the mammary gland, which contracts to project the milk deep into the throat of the calf when it comes up to the breast. The calf grows at a rate of one hundred kilos a day, and every day it grows several centimeters longer. And during all this time, the mother goes without eating, living on the reserves she has accumulated throughout the summer while she was straining out tons of krill in the cold ocean waters. She will start to eat again only when she and her young have returned to the polar zone.

When I saw them off Deception Island, the whales had just reached the end of their journey, a round trip of twenty thousand kilometers. These three were no dreamy-souled travelers: they had migrated for their own survival and that of the species, not for play. They had enacted a kind of rite that is millennia old. When they dived vertically, offering us the spectacle of their gigantic tail flukes, I believe I gauged the depth of our ignorance about them.

The field of study is still limitless. Why do species behave so differently one from the other, and why are there so many differences among populations of the same species? Why do individuals in the Southern Hemisphere grow larger than those in the Northern Hemisphere? We can determine the age of certain whales, some of which live to be eighty, by studying the buildup blocking their ears, but this is absent in other whales. Are whales born with a genetic memory of their ancestral migration routes? These are only a few among hundreds of questions. And every answer gives rise to new questions. The whale is full of enigmas. My colleague Richard Sears has ceaselessly studied them in the Saint-Laurent Estuary for twenty-five years now, attempting to equip them with electronic instruments, transmitters, and Argos tags, which permit him to follow them by satellite. But they always end up losing this equipment and disappear. Where do they go? Where do they come from? It's a mystery. There is something metaphysical about blue whales.

When the sea closed over the whales as they dived, I remember feeling a kind of retrospective fear. Whale hunting came very close to making the species extinct. If, starting in 1967, blue whales had not been protected, if the chase had continued for just one decade longer, no one would ever have had the joy of watching them again, as I had just done.

Ten years. Only ten years. The fate of the largest animal on the planet was played out in extremis. That of hundreds of other species is being played out today. The days are passing; the hours are fading away. And time, unfortunately, is not in their favor. Everything depends on us.

Epilogue
What if Tomorrow They Disappeared Forever?

While I was finishing this book, over a thousand specialists from fifty countries were getting ready to participate in a major event: the First World Conference on Marine Mammals in Monaco, organized by the Center for Research on Marine Mammals in La Rochelle. To be frank, I had sent in a proposal out of professional courtesy, and was not really sure I could make good on it. I was hoping that the Italian proposal would be chosen. Who doesn't dream of going to Venice? But my project was selected, and I had to assume the responsibility. It was a heavy task, but I ended up getting excited about it.

What is the purpose of such a conference? What were we going to discuss? I often think about how dolphins, whales, seals, sirenians, polar bears, and sea otters have no need of humans to live their lives. They did not wait around until the end of the second millennium to conquer the oceans; they were there long before humans.

And this is precisely the point. We need to act so they'll survive our presence. Given the way humans have colonized the planet, if we don't start paying more attention to what we do, soon there will be no more dolphins or whales or seals or sirenians or polar bears or sea otters.

If this initial conference could clarify the situation, if it could contribute to advancing our research, it would already be a very good thing. Every year, we better understand how marine mammals live and better take stock of the threats hanging over them. These questions are at the heart of every researcher's worries. But the threats are unfortunately too numerous and too complex for us to nourish the hope of finding a miracle solution.

The Mediterranean monk seal is a sad example: in spite of all the efforts scientists have made on its behalf, in spite of large subsidies from the European Union, it is on the verge of extinction. In a few years, the monk seal has nine out of ten "chances" of being definitively listed as a dead species. Monk seals were hunted up to World War II, not for commercial purposes, but simply because they "bothered" offshore fishermen by eating "their" fish, or getting tangled up in their nets. The last two French specimens were killed in Corsica in the 1970s. Then the proliferation of human activity along the coast forced them to abandon most of their mating grounds. Sea traffic, chemical pollution, construction along the shore near the caves where the females give birth, the exhaustion of fish stocks: rare today are places favorable to their survival. Only a few hundred monk seals now remain, on Greek and Turkish islands and along the coast of Mauritania. Illnesses are decimating the last colonies that still can reproduce. In one year alone, a virus killed more than three hundred seals on the African littoral, in a colony estimated to consist of four hundred individuals at most.

We know that the high level of pollution found in the

organs of seals is responsible for their weakened immune systems; the animals have become more susceptible to viruses, and no natural resistance can eradicate epizootic diseases. We have also recorded a drop in the birth rate and a higher rate of miscarriage in females contaminated with industrial and agricultural pollutants. If the seals are reproducing at a slower rate than normal, and if they are easily susceptible to viruses and mortal illness, we have to ask ourselves what kind of miracle it will take for the species to survive. It is horrible for scientists to be in a situation in which they are forced to admit their powerlessness, their inability to do anything when they're faced with a species condemned to certain death.

For some years now, we have noted that the species inhabiting coastal waters are the most threatened. The explanation is simple: the impact of human activity is stronger along the shore than on the open sea. Almost all marine mammals are under serious stress from intensified pollution, heavy sea traffic, and drastic overfishing. In numerous regions, they suffer other problems as well. The dolphins on the Indian subcontinent suffer from the construction of dams in the middle of their "territory"; like the baiji in China or the bouto of the Amazon, the dugong and the manatee fall victim to the propellers of outboard motors; whales that reproduce in the shelter of bays are harassed by whale-watching tourists; seals get caught in fishing nets.

I have already said this in these pages, but I must insist again and again that the pelagic trawl is an abomination. Four hundred meters wide and nine hundred meters deep: this is sheer madness! Why protest and outlaw drift nets if it is only to invent an even more devastating instrument? We are like the proverbial mad scientists in our treatment of the ocean. We have no right to drag the depths of the sea, then throw cartloads of fish overboard simply because we do not have the time to sort them. When the stocks of hake and anchovies have diminished to the point that it is useless to fish at all, it will be too late to get upset. The dolphins will have disappeared because nothing was left for them to eat. And the fishermen themselves can stay put on the dock. We are playing "scorched sea" politics, just like the "scorched earth" politics of yesterday.

Thousands of sea mammals are dying because of this headlong pursuit. When I see their cadavers, mutilated, ripped open, amputated of their tails, I am not only revolted by the agony these animals have suffered in their traps: I am horrified because this massacre announces a disaster. The really unbearable idea is that we are ruining our future by killing off everything around us. It is unreasonable, stupid, blind. We have already experienced such disasters elsewhere, and we are still suffering the consequences. Many fishermen know that this relentlessness is criminal: they no longer care for the sort of work that forces them to destroy the thing they love. The smell of rotting dolphins is intolerable to them. If we don't put a stop to this waste, we run the risk of having to live with the stench of it on our hands for decades, perhaps even centuries.

When dolphins, seals, and whales are in danger, so are all the flora and fauna in the ocean. And when the ocean is threatened, the planet is threatened—and this, of course, includes *Homo sapiens.* Marine mammals are at the top of the food chain; they concentrate all the problems and render them visible to our weak human eyes, which are blind underwater and terribly ignorant about what goes on beneath the surface. We know very little about marine mammals, and we are ignoramuses concerning crustaceans, mollusks, and fish. As for the microscopic organisms that make up plankton, the fundamental base of the entire food chain, our knowledge is nothing but an impressionistic blur. Scientists long ago discovered that cetaceans and pinnipeds are the best indicators of the oceans' health. Working to understand the predators, we thus diagnose the health of the sea. Does it have to be repeated again? The sea is sick. Very sick. But who worries when a sardine dies, who gets excited when a shrimp suffers, who is revolted when a squid suffocates? Several ecological associations have taken whales, seals, or dolphins as their symbols because they know that these favored animals will serve their cause well, unlike the wood louse or the spider, even if they, too, are endangered. But working to protect the planet cannot be reduced to saving a few of the superstars in the animal kingdom that we have turned into totems and myths because they stir our deepest emotions. If we do this, we risk overprotecting the species we love to the detriment of the others, those that are guilty only of not eliciting such feelings. To be sure that our children, too, will be filled with wonder by the animals we cherish, it is high time to worry about the equilibrium of these animals' environments and the health of their prey.

To end on a more optimistic note, it is enough to realize that human beings are at the origin of all the threats to endangered species, and thus we have the means to stop this hellish process. It is not inevitable. Nothing is uncontrollable. It is not a natural catastrophe that escapes our powers. We are the ones who have caused the damage. Do we have arms to destroy? Well, then, we also have tools to build. True hope comes in understanding that we have everything we need to take the situation in hand. But first we have to identify the major problems, admit the damage, stop averting our eyes, and above all stop trying to absolve ourselves by blaming a scapegoat. "Evil" industrialists, "ugly" farmers, "cruel" fishermen, and incompetent politicians are not at fault. You and I together consume the products of industry, agriculture, and fishing. You and I together elect the politicians. You and I together can make things go in the right direction.

There are thousands of ways to inflect a curve, get on our feet again, modify daily habits, pay more attention to the education of those who tomorrow will hold the reins of power. It is possible to think a little more carefully about consequences before we act. My role is not to give lessons or hand out "recipes." We all know very well how to better the situation at the individual level. I don't pretend to know better than you the right way to go about things. My responsibility is to sound the alarm, because I can't stand the thought that tomorrow there may be no more dolphins in the Bay of Biscay or anywhere else. Perhaps my function is only to convey my wonder at the beauty and richness of our planet by telling stories about whales and dolphins. To my way of thinking, it is the best way to awaken motivation. But if we want to be able to tell more stories tomorrow, it is urgent to open our eyes today.

Species List

The classification of cetaceans into taxonomic categories is still subject to changes that reflect our rather poor knowledge of and uncertainties about this order of mammals. The Society for Marine Mammalogy (SMM) has recently published a revised list including new scientific names (*Histriophoca fasciata* instead of *Phoca fasciata*) and new species formerly considered as subspecies (for example, the Antarctic minke whale) or vice versa (the Ganges and the Indus river dolphins are now grouped within a single species of South Asian river dolphin).[1] Nevertheless, the International Whaling Commission (IWC) has not adopted all of these changes for their new listing of cetaceans.[2] The list proposed below is based on the IWC nomenclature for cetaceans and on the SMM list for pinnipeds and sirenians.

---

1. Dale W. Rice, *Marine Mammals of the World: Systematics and Distribution.* Society for Marine Mammalogy, Special Publication 4, 1998 (231 pp).

2. Decision taken at the International Whaling Commission conference in Auckland, Australia, July 2000.

Scientific Name	Common Name
Order	
Cetacea (82 species)	**cetaceans**
Suborder	
Mysticeti (13 species)	**baleen whales**
Family	
Eschrichtiidae (1 species)	**gray whales**
Eschrichtius robustus	gray whale
Family	
Balaenopteridae (7 species)	**balaenopterids, rorqual whales**
Balaenoptera acutorostrata	common minke whale
Balaenoptera bonaerensis	Antarctic minke whale
Balaenoptera edeni	Bryde's whale
Balaenoptera borealis	sei whale
Balaenoptera physalus	fin whale
Balaenoptera musculus	blue whale
Megaptera novaeangliae	humpback whale
Family	
Balaenidae (4 species)	**right whales**
Eubalaena glacialis	North Atlantic right whale
Eubalaena australis	southern right whale
Eubalaena japonica	North Pacific right whale
Balaena mysticetus	bowhead whale
Family	
Neobalaenidae (1 species)	**pygmy right whales**
Caperea marginata	pygmy right whale

Suborder
Odontoceti (69 species)　　**tooth whales**

Family
Iniidae (1 species)　　**iniids**
　Inia geoffrensis　　boto, bouto

Family
Lipotidae (1 species)　　**Lipotids**
　Lipotes vexillifer　　baiji, beiji

Family
Pontoporiidae (1 species)　　**pontoporids**
　Pontoporia blainvillei　　franciscana

Family
Platanistidae (1 species)　　**platanistids**
　Platanista gangetica　　susu, South Asian river dolphin

Family
Delphinidae (34 species)　　**delphinids**
　Steno bredanensis　　rough-toothed dolphin

　Sousa chinensis　　Indo-Pacific humpback dolphin

　Sousa teuszii　　Atlantic humpback dolphin

　Sotalia fluviatilis　　tucuxi

　Tursiops truncatus　　common bottlenose dolphin

　Tursiops aduncus　　Indo-Pacific bottlenose dolphin

　Stenella longirostris　　spinner dolphin, long-snouted spinner dolphin

Stenella attenuata (dubia)	pantropical spotted dolphin
Stenella frontalis (plagiodon)	Atlantic spotted dolphin
Stenella clymene	Clymene dolphin, short-snouted spinner dolphin
Stenella coeruleoalba	striped dolphin
Delphinus delphis	short-beaked common dolphin
Delphinus capensis	long-beaked common dolphin
Lagenodelphis hosei	Fraser's dolphin
Lagenorhynchus albirostris	white-beaked dolphin
Lagenorhynchus acutus	Atlantic white-sided dolphin
Lagenorhynchus obliquidens	Pacific white-sided dolphin
Lagenorhynchus obscurus	dusky dolphin
Lagenorhynchus australis	Peale's dolphin
Lagenorhynchus cruciger	hourglass dolphin
Cephalorhynchus commersonii	Commerson's dolphin
Cephalorhynchus eutropia	Chilean dolphin, black dolphin
Cephalorhynchus heavisidii	Heaviside's dolphin
Cephalorhynchus hectori	Hector's dolphin
Lissodelphis borealis	northern right whale dolphin
Lissodelphis peronii	southern right whale dolphin
Grampus griseus	Risso's dolphin
Peponocephala electra	melon-headed whale

Feresa attenuata	pygmy killer whale
Pseudorca crassidens	false killer whale
Globicephala melas	long-finned pilot whale
Globicephala macrorhynchus	short-finned pilot whale
Orcinus orca	killer whale
Orcaella brevirostris	Irrawaddy dolphin

Family
Phocoenidae (6 species)   **porpoises**

Phocoena phocoena	harbor porpoise, common porpoise
Phocoena sinus	vaquita, cochito
Phocoena spinipinnis	Burmeister's porpoise
Phocoena dioptrica	spectacled porpoise
Neophocaena phocaenoides	finless porpoise
Phocoenoides dalli	Dall's porpoise

Family
Monodontidae (2 species)   **monodontids**

Delphinapterus leucas	white whale, beluga
Monodon monoceros	narwhal

Family
Physeteridae (1 species)   **sperm whales**

Physeter macrocephalus	sperm whale

Family
Kogiidae (2 species)   **pygmy sperm whales**

Kogia breviceps	pygmy sperm whale
Kogia sima (simus)	dwarf sperm whale

Family
Ziphiidae (20 species)   **beaked whales**

  Berardius arnuxii   Arnoux's beaked whale
  Berardius bairdii   Baird's beaked whale

  Ziphius cavirostris   Cuvier's beaked whale

  Tasmacetus shepherdi   Shepherd's beaked whale, Tasman beaked whale

  Hyperoodon ampullatus   northern bottlenose whale
  Hyperoodon planifrons   southern bottlenose whale

  Indopacetus pacificus   Longman's beaked whale

  Mesoplodon bahamondi   Bahamonde's beaked whale
  Mesoplodon peruvianus   pygmy beaked whale, lesser beaked whale

  Mesoplodon hectori   Hector's beaked whale
  Mesoplodon mirus   True's beaked whale
  Mesoplodon europaeus   Gervais' beaked whale
  Mesoplodon ginkgodens   ginkgo-toothed beaked whale

  Mesoplodon grayi   Gray's beaked whale
  Mesoplodon carlhubbsi   Hubbs' beaked whale
  Mesoplodon bowdoini   Andrew's beaked whale
  Mesoplodon stejnegeri   Stejneger's beaked whale
  Mesoplodon bidens   Sowerby's beaked whale
  Mesoplodon layardii   strap-toothed whale, Layard's beaked whale

  Mesoplodon densirostris   Blainville's beaked whale

Order
Carnivora   **carnivora**

Suborder
Pinnipedia (36 species)   **pinnipeds**

Family
Odobenidae (1 species)   **odobenids**
 Odobenus rosmarus   walrus

Family
Otaridae (16 species)   **otarids**
 Phocarctos hookeri   New Zealand sea lion,
                                     Hooker's sea lion

 Otaria flavescens (byronia)   South American sea lion,
                                     southern sea lion

 Zalophus californianus   California sea lion
 Zalophus japonicus   Japanese sea lion
 Zalophus wollebaeki   Galápagos sea lion

 Neophoca cinerea   Australian sea lion,
                                     Auckland sea lion

 Eumetopias jubatus   northern sea lion,
                                     Steller sea lion

 Callorhinus ursinus   northern fur seal

 Arctocephalus pusillus   South African fur seal,
                                     Cape/Australian/Tasmanian
                                     fur seal
 Arctocephalus gazella   Antarctic fur seal,
                                     Kerguelen fur seal
 Arctocephalus forsteri   New Zealand fur seal,
                                     Australasian fur seal
 Arctocephalus tropicalis   subantarctic fur seal,
                                     Amsterdam Island fur seal

Arctocephalus australis	South American fur seal
Arctocephalus galapagoensis	Galápagos fur seal
Arctocephalus philippii	Juan Fernández fur seal
Arctocephalus townsendi	Guadalupe fur seal

Family

Phocidae (19 species)   **true seals**

Phoca vitulina	harbor seal, common seal
Phoca largha	spotted seal, larga seal
Pusa (Phoca) hispida	ringed seal, natchik
Pusa (Phoca) sibirica	Baikal seal
Pusa (Phoca) caspica	Caspian seal
Pagophilus (Phoca) groenlandica	harp seal, Greenland seal
Histriophoca (Phoca) fasciata	ribbon seal
Halichoerus grypus	gray seal, Atlantic seal
Erignathus barbatus	bearded seal, ugruk
Cystophora cristata	hooded seal
Monachus monachus	Mediterranean monk seal
Monachus tropicalis	Caribbean monk seal, West Indian monk seal
Monachus schauinslandi	Hawaiian monk seal
Lobodon carcinophaga	crabeater seal
Ommatophoca rossii	Ross seal
Hydrurga leptonyx	leopard seal
Leptonychotes weddellii	Weddell seal

| *Mirounga leonina* | southern elephant seal |
| *Mirounga angustirostris* | northern elephant seal |

Order
Sirenia (5 species)   **sirenians**

Family
Dugongidae (2 species)   **dugongs and sea cows**

| *Dugong dugong* | dugong |
| *Hydrodamalis gigas* | Steller's sea cow, Rhytina |

Family
Trichechidae (3 species)   **manatees**

Trichechus manatus	Caribbean manatee, West Indian manatee
Trichechus senegalensis	African manatee, West African manatee
Trichechus inunguis	Amazon manatee

Other marine mammals

Order
Carnivora   **carnivora**

Family
Mustelidae (2 species)   **mustelids**

| *Enhydra lutris* | sea otter |
| *Lutra felina* | marine otter, chungungo |

Family
Ursidae (1 species)   **ursids**

| *Ursus maritimus* | polar bear |

Glossary

Baleen plates: plates or strips of hornlike material also known as whalebone, found in the upper jaws of Mysticeti, or baleen whales. When they are pressed together, baleen plates form a filter that retains food and lets water escape.

Blowhole: an orifice or nostril, situated on the top of the head, through which cetaceans breathe. Members of the tooth whale suborder have a single blowhole; in baleen whales, it is double.

Blubber: a layer of fat between the skin and muscles of whales and other marine mammals. Blubber acts as an insulator by slowing down the exchange between the temperature of the body and that of the exterior environment.

Breach: a leap of a whale or other cetacean from the water. Also used as a verb: to breach.

Callosities: callused patches on right whales, usually found on the head, where small crustaceans attach themselves to the skin.

Caudal (adj.): near the tail or hind parts.

Capelin: a small, edible fish similar to a smelt, found in the North Atlantic Ocean and the North Pacific Ocean.

Cetacean: the order of mammals made up of baleen whales and tooth whales, including eighty-two species of dolphins, whales, and porpoises.

Center for Research on Marine Mammals: Centre de Recherche sur les Mammifères Marins, located in La Rochelle, France.

Corvette: a small, fast warship usually armed with a single tier of guns.

Dolphin: any of the thirty-four species of marine mammals belonging to the family Delphinidae. Classed under the suborder of tooth whales, dolphins are usually smaller than whales and distinguished by a beaklike snout.

Drift net: a fishing net of variable size that is suspended between buoys and allowed to drift with the current for several hours at a time.

Epizootic: said of a disease that simultaneously attacks many members of a large group of animals.

Flipper: a wide, flat limb used for swimming by dolphins, whales, and other sea mammals. Front flippers resembling fins help animals change direction and stabilize themselves in the water.

Fluke: one of the triangular, horizontal divisions in the tail of a whale or dolphin.

GPS: U.S. Global Positioning System, a navigational aid for precisely locating positions via satellite.

Homoeothermic: warm-blooded. Said of an animal that produces its own heat in order to maintain a constant body temperature independent of environmental temperature. Mammals and birds are homoeothermic.

Hydrodynamics: the study of forces acting upon or exerted by liquids. There is a hydrodynamic relationship between the shape of an animal's body and the resistance it encounters when it moves through water.

Keratin: a protective, fibrous protein forming the outer layer of epidermal structures found, for example, in hair, bone, and claws.

Krill: small marine crustaceans or planktonic shrimp, which make up the major part of baleen whales' diet. Latin name: *Euphosia superba.*

Melon: the convex front part of a tooth whale's head. The melon is full of oil, called spermaceti in sperm whales, which mainly serves to concentrate the sound waves the animal produces.

Mysticete (Mysticeti, pl.): the suborder of cetaceans known as baleen whales or whalebone whales, which have plates of baleen or whalebone and no teeth. Rorquals, right whales, and the gray whale are among the thirteen species of Mysticeti.

Odontocete (Odontoceti, pl.): the suborder of cetaceans known as tooth whales, which have teeth. Freshwater and oceanic dolphins, porpoises, sperm whales, beaked whales, the narwal, and the beluga are among the sixty-nine species of Odontoceti.

Pelagic: referring to the open sea, as opposed to coastal or inland waters.

Pelagic trawl: a metal-webbed fishing net shaped like a funnel used for deep-sea fishing. It is dragged by one or two ships for several hours at a time and reaches a depth of several hundred meters.

Pinniped: a member of the suborder Pinnipedia, carnivorous marine mammals. Walruses, sea lions, and seals are among the thirty-six species of pinnipeds.

Plankton: microscopic plant and animal organisms floating in freshwater or saltwater, found in large groups known as banks.

Porpoise: any of the six species of cetaceans belonging to the family Phocoenidae, characterized by a blunt snout and a triangular dorsal fin.

Race: a subspecies. Used to describe a plant or animal population that has lived in a distinct geographical region long enough for the frequency of inherited traits to distinguish it from other members of the same species.

Rorqual: any of the baleen whales belonging to the genus *Balaenoptera,* characterized by longitudinal throat grooves and a small, pointed dorsal fin. Rorqual whales include the seven species of the family Balaenopterids.

Rostrum: the beak or snout of a porpoise, dolphin, or whale.

Sirenian: any of the five species of the order sirenia, herbivorous marine mammals including the dugong and the manatee.

Sonar: SO[und] NA[vigation] R[anging]. A system that uses the transmission and reflection of sound waves to detect and locate objects underwater.

Species: the category of taxonomic classification ranking under genus, consisting of individuals capable of breeding with each other. The names of species are made up of a Latin genus name followed by an epithet or adjective, as in *Balaenoptera musculus* (blue whale).

Spermaceti: a very fine, white, oily substance found in the melon of sperm whales. Its name comes from its resemblance to sperm.

Stranded: used to describe marine mammals found washed up or beached on shore. In the case of cetaceans like whales, dolphins, and porpoises, the animals are usually dead, but if they are pinnipeds, like seals, sea lions, and walruses, they often are still alive.

Metric Measurement Conversion Table

Swimming with Giants uses metric measurements because that is the standard within the scientific community. For those readers more familiar with standard U.S. measurements, we have provided the following conversion table.

Unit	Number of Meters	Approximate U.S. Equivalent
kilometer	1,000	0.62 miles/3,280 feet
meter	1	39.37 inches/3.28 feet
centimeter	0.01	0.39 inches

Unit	Number of Square Meters	Approximate U.S. Equivalent
square kilometer	1,000,000	0.3861 square miles
square meter	1	10.75 square feet
square centimeter	0.0001	0.155 square inches

Unit	Number of Grams	Approximate U.S. Equivalent
metric ton	1,000,000	1.102 short tons
kilogram	1,000	2.2046 pounds
gram	1	0.035 ounces

Unit	Number of Liters	Approximate U.S. Liquid Equivalent
dekaliter	10	2.64 gallons
liter	1	1.057 quarts

0 degrees Celsius = 32 degrees Fahrenheit
100 degrees Celsius = 212 degrees Fahrenheit

ANNE COLLET directs the Center for Research on Marine Mammals (CRMM) in La Rochelle, and the France-Europe Department of the National Center for the Study of Marine Mammals. Early recognized for her outstanding research on the reproduction of dolphins, Dr. Collet is internationally known today as one of the experts on cetacean studies. She has fulfilled many functions in French and international organizations, including scientific expert for the International Whaling Commission, and has served on the boards of the European Cetacean Society and the Society for Marine Biology. In addition to her numerous scientific publications, she is the author of *Baleines, un enjeu écologique,* with G. Ross and B. Saladin D'Anglure (Editions Autrement, 1999), *Les Dauphins, historique et biologie,* with R. Duguy (Editions du Rocher, 1987), and *Vie et mort des baleines,* with Yves Cohat (Gallimard, 2000). *Swimming with Giants* was originally published as *Dance avec les baleines* (Plon, 1998).

More Books on The World As Home
from Milkweed Editions

To order books or for more information,
contact Milkweed at (800) 520-6455
or visit our websites
(www.milkweed.org / www.worldashome.org).

Brown Dog of the Yaak:
Essays on Art and Activism
Rick Bass

Writing the Sacred into the Real
Alison Hawthorne Deming

Boundary Waters:
The Grace of the Wild
Paul Gruchow

Grass Roots:
The Universe of Home
Paul Gruchow

The Necessity of Empty Places
Paul Gruchow

A Sense of the Morning:
Field Notes of a Born Observer
David Brendan Hopes

Taking Care:
Thoughts on Storytelling and Belief
William Kittredge

The Barn at the End of the World:
The Apprenticeship of a Quaker, Buddhist Shepherd
Mary Rose O'Reilley

Walking the High Ridge:
Life As Field Trip
Robert Michael Pyle

Ecology of a Cracker Childhood
Janisse Ray

The Dream of the Marsh Wren:
Writing As Reciprocal Creation
Pattiann Rogers

The Country of Language
Scott Russell Sanders

Of Landscape and Longing:
Finding a Home at the Water's Edge
Carolyn Servid

The Book of the Tongass
Edited by Carolyn Servid and Donald Snow

Homestead
Annick Smith

Testimony:
Writers of the West Speak On Behalf of Utah Wilderness
Compiled by Stephen Trimble and Terry Tempest Williams

Shaped by Wind and Water:
Reflections of a Naturalist
Ann Haymond Zwinger

Other books of interest to The World As Home readers

ESSAYS

Eccentric Islands:
Travels Real and Imaginary
Bill Holm

The Heart Can Be Filled Anywhere on Earth:
Minneota, Minnesota
Bill Holm

Shedding Life:
Disease, Politics, and Other Human Conditions
Miroslav Holub

CHILDREN'S NOVELS

Tides
V. M. Caldwell

No Place
Kay Haugaard

The Monkey Thief
Aileen Kilgore Henderson

Treasure of Panther Peak
Aileen Kilgore Henderson

The Dog with Golden Eyes
Frances Wilbur

CHILDREN'S ANTHOLOGIES

Stories from Where We Live— The North Atlantic Coast
Edited by Sara St. Antoine

ANTHOLOGIES

Sacred Ground:
Writings about Home
Edited by Barbara Bonner

Urban Nature:
Poems about Wildlife in the City
Edited by Laure-Anne Bosselaar

Verse and Universe:
Poems about Science and Mathematics
Edited by Kurt Brown

POETRY

Turning Over the Earth
Ralph Black

Boxelder Bug Variations
Bill Holm

Butterfly Effect
Harry Humes

Eating Bread and Honey
Pattiann Rogers

Firekeeper:
New and Selected Poems
Pattiann Rogers

The World As Home, the nonfiction publishing program of Milkweed Editions, is dedicated to exploring our relationship to the natural world. Not espousing any particular environmentalist or political agenda, these books are a forum for distinctive literary writing that not only alerts the reader to vital issues but also offers personal testimonies to living harmoniously with other species in urban, rural, and wilderness communities.

Milkweed Editions publishes with the intention of making a humane impact on society, in the belief that literature is a transformative art uniquely able to convey the essential experiences of the human heart and spirit. To that end, Milkweed publishes distinctive voices of literary merit in handsomely designed, visually dynamic books, exploring the ethical, cultural, and esthetic issues that free societies need continually to address. Milkweed Editions is a not-for-profit press.

Interior design by Donna Burch
Typeset in Centaur
by Stanton Publication Services, Inc.
Printed on acid-free, 55# Perfection Antique Recycled paper
by Maple-Vail Book Manufacturing